PENGUIN BOOKS

HALLIWELL'S MOVIE QUIZ

Leslie Halliwell was born in Bolton, England. He buys most of the feature films and series screened by the ITV network in England and goes twice a year to Hollywood in search of them. He has been an enthusiast for the medium since childhood and wishes he had spent more time in Hollywood during its golden years. Mr Halliwell spent several years as film reviewer for *Picturegoer* and *Sight and Sound* and has contributed to other publications in England, including *The Spectator, Films and Filming*, and *The Times Literary Supplement*. His other books include *The Filmgoer's Companion, Mountain of Dreams, The Filmgoer's Book of Quotes*, and *The Clapperboard Book of the Cinema*.

Halliwell's Movie Quiz

by LESLIE HALLIWELL

PENGUIN BOOKS

Penguin Books Ltd, Harmondsworth,
Middlesex, England
Penguin Books, 625 Madison Avenue,
New York, New York 10022, U.S.A.
Penguin Books Australia Ltd, Ringwood,
Victoria, Australia
Penguin Books Canada Limited, 2801 John Street,
Markham, Ontario, Canada L3R 1B4
Penguin Books (N.Z.) Ltd, 182-190 Wairau Road,
Auckland 10, New Zealand

First published in Great Britain by
Everest Books Ltd 1977
First published in the United States of America by
Penguin Books 1978

LIBRARY OF CONGRESS CATALOGING IN PUBLICATION DATA
Halliwell, Leslie.
    Halliwell's movie quiz.
    1.Moving-pictures — Miscellanea.   I. Title.
II. Title: Movie quiz.
PN1993.85.H3 1978   791.43   78-9312
ISBN 0 14 00.4937 1

Printed in the United States of America by
Offset Paperback Mfrs., Inc., Dallas, Pennsylvania
Set in Plantin

FOREWORD

Movie quizzes come and go, but the complaint of real film buffs is always that they're too easy. Well, here's one that isn't; and it's a big one. Three thousand five hundred questions, broken up into quiz papers labelled easy, medium and difficult . . . but even the easy ones assume a reasonable knowledge of movies new and old, and some of the difficult ones are real brain twisters for addicts with long and accurate memories. Hopefully you'll think the answers are worth working for – you'll certainly pick up a fair amount of useful information along the way.

The questions are so designed that there can only be one correct answer, and it's always a fact rather than an opinion.

A scorecard is provided. If you get a thousand correct answers you're doing pretty well and can count yourself a fan of some dedication. Two thousand, and you ought to win an Oscar – likewise if you get every question right in a quiz labelled difficult. Two thousand five hundred, and you should have written the book yourself.

EXPLANATORY NOTE

This quiz is for film buffs, and no apology is made for that fact. The fact that a quiz is labelled "easy" therefore means that it should be easy for a film buff with a good memory, not for the casual filmgoer or telewatcher.

A few questions here and there are repeated, especially in the closing test paper. This is deliberate! The fact that you discover something on page thirteen does not necessarily mean that you can remember it on page one hundred and eight, although it is to your advantage to do so as you will pick up an extra mark.

Keep your score by checking the open square beside each answer you get right, and transfer your tally for each of the quizzes to the scorecard at the front of the answer section. This will make it easy to arrive at your final count. If it helps your pride, let me say that I believe no one in the world could answer every question correctly: we are all specialists in our own way and can't know everything. I think I myself might have got a score of around 2250, and quite a lot of people could equal that. I am constantly amazed at the extent of movie knowledge possessed by fans who write to me, especially young people who must have relied entirely on television for their movie education.

Here is an aimless romp through the classics of film history. It should be fairly simple for any keen student, and is in fact the easiest quiz in the book . . . a good way to get a lot of points under your belt.

1 In what city was NINOTCHKA set?

2 Who directed HOW GREEN WAS MY VALLEY?

3 Name the film in which Greta Garbo played a mistress of Napoleon.

4 Name the classic silent western directed in 1923 by James Cruze.

5 What D. W. Griffith film was based on a novel called THE CHINK AND THE CHILD?

6 Whose first film as a director was THE PLEASURE GARDEN (1926)?

7 Who produced and directed THE PRIVATE LIFE OF HENRY VIII?

8 Who co-wrote CITIZEN KANE with Orson Welles?

9 In THE GREAT DICTATOR, Charles Chaplin played Hynkel, but who played Napaloni?

10 Name the Walt Disney feature cartoon in which Leopold Stokowski conducted "a sound track concert with accompanying images".

11 Name the film in which Gary Cooper played Lou Gehrig the baseball star.

12 Who directed BRIEF ENCOUNTER?

13 Which "ROAD" is missing? SINGAPORE, ZANZIBAR, MOROCCO, RIO, BALI, HONG KONG.

14 Name the film directed by Vittorio de Sica about slum dwellers escaping into the skies on broomsticks.

15 Who wrote the screenplay of GONE WITH THE WIND?

16 Famous photographer Karl Freund directed only two films, in 1932 and 1935, both in the horror field. Name them.

17 Name the director of STRIKE, THE GENERAL LINE, and ALEXANDER NEVSKY.

18 By what name is William Henry Pratt better known?

19 Name the Academy Award winning short in which Laurel and Hardy spend three reels getting a piano up a flight of steps.

20 Who played the title role (the doctor) in THE CABINET OF DR CALIGARI?

21 What comedy team first appeared in ONE NIGHT IN THE TROPICS?

22 The stage and film musical of the seventies, A LITTLE NIGHT MUSIC, is based on what film by Ingmar Bergman?

23 Who played Chorus in HENRY V?

24 Fine documentaries of World War Two, LISTEN TO BRITAIN and FIRES WERE STARTED, were directed by who?

25 Everyone knows Erich Maria Remarque's ALL QUIET ON THE WESTERN FRONT; but can you name the sequel, filmed by Universal in 1957?

26 Who played Albert to Anna Neagle's Victoria in VICTORIA THE GREAT and SIXTY GLORIOUS YEARS?

27 Who had eight credits on IN WHICH WE SERVE, including writer and director?

28 Mickey Mouse, Goofy and Pluto are known the world
    over, but can you name Mickey's horsy friend who
    appeared in the early thirties?

29 Pola Negri appeared as Catherine the Great in what
    1924 film by Ernst Lubitsch?

30 Who was the Ringo Kid in STAGECOACH?

31 Name the two missing dwarfs: Happy, Bashful,
    Sneezy, Sleepy, Dopey . . .

32 Who photographed THE MAGNIFICENT AMBER-
    SONS?

33 Name the 1947 film in which Charles Chaplin played a
    multiple murderer.

34 What popular 1937 film (starring among others
    Fernandel, Raimu, Pierre Blanchar and Harry Baur)
    gave director Julien Duvivier his ticket to Hollywood?

35 While there he made a pretty close remake of his great
    success. Name it and the actress who played the title
    role.

36 In what film did Alec Guinness play eight parts?

37 Name the film in which Jacques Tati played a postman?

38 What was the first CARRY ON?

39 The Marx Brothers made one film which was a recog-
    nisable version of a Broadway straight comedy. Name
    it.

40 Name also the remake starring Frank Sinatra.

41 What star's films included TUMBLEWEED, WHITE
    OAK and WILD BILL HICKOK?

12 Who directed ONE FLEW OVER THE CUCKOO'S
    NEST?

43 What 1934 comedy won Oscars for both its stars?

44 In what film did George Raft first spin a coin, a trick that half the world imitated?

45 Who played the title role in BABY FACE NELSON in 1957?

46 Who played Dr Watson to Peter Cushing's Sherlock Holmes in the 1957 HOUND OF THE BASKER-VILLES?

47 Who played the villainous husband in the British 1940 version of GASLIGHT?

48 Who directed, among many others, ONLY ANGELS HAVE WINGS, BRINGING UP BABY and THE BIG SLEEP?

49 Who was first known as Marjorie Robertson?

50 Who wrote the music and lyrics for TOP HAT?

51 Who were jokingly known as The Singing Capon and The Iron Butterfly?

52 In what film did Cyd Charisse take over a role from Greta Garbo?

53 What was Fritz Lang's first American film?

54 What company made BALLET OOP, WILLIE THE KID and MADELEINE?

55 Who played Wilson in WILSON?

56 In which Marxian frolic did all the brothers impersonate Maurice Chevalier?

57 In 1929 John Grierson made what is sometimes inaccurately called the first documentary. Name it.

58 Who directed AN ITALIAN STRAW HAT?

59 In which film did Rudolph Valentino play a Cossack lieutenant in imperial Russia?

60 On whose novel was WHISKY GALORE (TIGHT LITTLE ISLAND) based?

61 Who played Edgar Linton in Willam Wyler's WUTHERING HEIGHTS?

62 Name the film by Michael Powell and Emeric Pressburger in which David Farrar played a bomb disposal expert with a drink problem.

63 With which Hitchcock film do you associate the Merry Widow waltz?

64 By what well-known studio was THE MAN IN THE WHITE SUIT made?

65 THE SUN SHINES BRIGHT was a 1953 remake of a 1934 film starring what actor?

66 The title of the 1934 film was the name of the character played by that actor. Name it.

67 What film by Elia Kazan documented the unsolved New England case of the murder of a clergyman?

68 Name the short ghost story film made by Michael MacLiammoir and Hilton Edwards during one of the frequent pauses in the filming of Orson Welles' OTHELLO.

69 In what Lubitsch film did the hero say? "Waiter, you see that moon? I want to see that moon in the champagne . . ."

70 What Busby Berkeley film contains the song I ONLY HAVE EYES FOR YOU?

71 Whose films include A CHAIRY TALE, PAS DE DEUX and BEGONE DULL CARE?

72 What musical involves a search for Miss Turnstiles?

73 Who was the supervisor of the WHY WE FIGHT series?

74 What was historically significant about TOOT, WHISTLE, PLUNK AND BOOM?

75 Who starred in BLOSSOM TIME?

76 Who played a bit part as a hungry diner in the 1929 silent film PICCADILLY?

77 Who directed MAN OF ARAN?

78 Whose autobiography is called BULLS, BALLS, BICYCLES AND ACTORS?

79 Who played Chauvelin in the 1934 THE SCARLET PIMPERNEL?

80 Who played Sanders in the 1935 SANDERS OF THE RIVER?

81 In what British comedy of 1938 are the romantic leads eaten by a bear in Kent?

82 Who wrote a history of the cinema called THE LIVELIEST ART?

83 Name the director of A PROPOS DE NICE, ZERO DE CONDUITE and L'ATALANTE?

84 Name the producer of FOREIGN CORRES-PONDENT, ALGIERS and the Elizabeth Taylor CLEOPATRA?

85 What affliction was suffered by Gerald McBoing Boing?

86 With what branch of cinema do you associate Bob Godfrey, Richard Williams and Ub Iwerks?

87 Who directed DIE DREIGROSCHENOPER?

88 Who starred in THE BLACK SHEEP OF WHITE-HALL, THE GOOSE STEPS OUT and MY LEARNED FRIEND?

89 Whose films include DROLE DE DRAME, QUAI DES BRUMES, LE JOIR SE LEVE and JENNY?

90 Name the brothers who invented a camera/projector and gave the first moving picture show to the public in 1895.

91 Whose films include FEET FIRST, HOT WATER and THE FRESHMAN?

92 What studio has for its trademark a mountain encircled by stars?

93 To whom was Carole Lombard married when she died?

94 Who appeared in TWICE TWO, HELPMATES and MEN O'WAR?

95 Name the all-star musical made in 1943 about sailors on leave in a big studio and the stars putting on a show for them. (Victor Moore played Eddie Bracken's father.)

96 What was the studio?

97 What film was made in 1932 with Irene Dunne and John Boles and in 1941 with Margaret Sullavan and Charles Boyer?

98 Of what film, also starring Clark Gable, was MOGAMBO a remake?

99 For what was George Melies best known?

100 Who wrote the music score for THE ADVENTURES OF ROBIN HOOD and KINGS ROW?

101 Who starred in HI NELLIE, THE WORLD CHANGES, and WE ARE NOT ALONE?

102 Who was Valentino's leading lady in THE SHEIK?

103 Who played Doc Holliday in MY DARLING CLEMENTINE?

104 And who played Pat Garrett in THE OUTLAW?

105 As what TV series character did Adam West become famous?

106 THE GLASS KEY, THE THIN MAN, THE DAIN CURSE, THE MALTESE FALCON. These Dashiell Hammett novels have all been filmed. Right or wrong?

107 Name the SIX MILLION DOLLAR MAN: his real name and his character name.

108 Hitler commissioned a film of the 1934 party congress at Nuremberg. As propaganda it succeeded beyond his wildest dreams. What is its title (in English) and who directed it?

109 Who directed THE DIARY OF ANNE FRANK?

110 Who played the old man in WILD STRAWBERRIES?

111 In what film did the Ale and Quail Club feature?

112 What great star of the silents also starred in a 1974 TV movie called KILLER BEES?

113 Who got his comeuppance in THE MAGNIFICENT AMBERSONS?

114 Name the film about the Brontes which starred Ida Lupino, Olivia de Havilland and Nancy Coleman.

115 Who was hailed as the film industry's first centenarian?

116 Name the cinematographer of CITIZEN KANE, THE GRAPES OF WRATH and THE BEST YEARS OF OUR LIVES.

117 Who played CITIZEN KANE as a child? And who played his son?

118 What was the subject of GENTLEMAN'S AGREEMENT?

119 Whose autobiography was FUN IN A CHINESE LAUNDRY?

120 In what film did Laurel and Hardy deceive their wives and go to a Chicago convention?

121 What other comedian did they meet there?

122 What social and historical distinction was given to A MATTER OF LIFE AND DEATH (STAIRWAY TO HEAVEN)?

123 Who starred in THE GREEN GODDESS, THE MAN WHO PLAYED GOD, THE IRON DUKE and VOLTAIRE?

124 Who wrote the script of MY LITTLE CHICKADEE?

125 Who was the first Tarzan?

126 Who was the *second* James Bond? (Don't count CASINO ROYALE)

127 What was Ingrid Bergman's first American film?

128 Who was D. W. Griffith's chief cameraman?

129 What is the film which Griffith is said to have directed in 1939 although it is credited to Hal Roach?

130 What film was alleged at various times to have been directed by Orson Welles or Howard Hawks, though credited to Christian Nyby?

131 What film starring Rudolph Valentino was remade with Bob Hope?

132 Chaplin and others made films for the Essanay company. How was the word Essanay devised?

133 In what film did Tony Curtis play The Great Leslie?

134 Who directed THE WAGES OF FEAR?

135 For what film did Harold Russell win an Academy Award, and what role did he play?

136 What was Clifton Webb's character name in SITTING PRETTY?

137 Who were the co-stars of MOTHER WORE TIGHTS?

138 Who played the murdered Jew in CROSSFIRE?

139 In what MGM film of 1940 was the song "Mr Gallagher and Mr Shean" performed?

140 Al Shean played himself, but who played "Mr Gallagher"?

141 In what film did Elizabeth Taylor disguise herself as a boy? (Mickey Rooney was also in it.)

142 What was the sequel to CLAUDIA?

143 The Trolley Song comes from what movie?

144 In the same film, who played the heroine's mother and father?

145 Of whose death did Joan Fontaine think Cary Grant guilty in SUSPICION?

146 Who played Dolittle in PYGMALION?

147 Who played Lennie in OF MICE AND MEN?

148 What was Charles Boyer's character name in ALGIERS?

149 Roland Young was TOPPER, but who was Mrs Topper?

150 Who played Moses in the 1923 De Mille version of
THE TEN COMMANDMENTS?

151 Who played Robert Cummings' grandmother in
KINGS ROW?

152 The silent version of THE PHANTOM OF THE
OPERA was directed by who?

153 Who played the leading role of Jim Apperson in
THE BIG PARADE?

154 Who directed it?

155 Who played his first leading role in THE WINNING
OF BARBARA WORTH?

156 What actor was born in New York, made his name in
Germany, was successful in American silent films but
returned to Germany when sound came?

157 Who directed THE JAZZ SINGER?

158 To whom did the production company Cosmopolitan
belong?

159 Who made THE OLD MILL, FLOWERS AND
TREES and MERBABIES?

160 What famous film runs 220 minutes?

161 For which company did music arranger Leo F.
Forbstein mainly work during the thirties?

162 And with which company do you associate the scores of
Joseph Gershenson?

163 In which film did Gene Kelly dance with a cartoon
mouse?

164 In which film did Esther Williams swim with Tom
and Jerry?

17

165 Who played the title role in LAURA?

166 DOUBLE INDEMNITY was remade as a TV movie in 1973. Who played the MacMurray/Stanwyck roles?

167 In what film were Danny Kaye's leading ladies Constance Dowling and Dinah Shore?

168 In what film was Sheridan Whiteside a leading character?

169 Who played Apple Annie in LADY FOR A DAY?

170 Name the 1960 remake starring Bette Davis.

171 Of what adventure film was Carl Denham the leading character?

172 Who played Humpty Dumpty in the 1933 ALICE IN WONDERLAND?

173 What was Mary Pickford's last film?

174 What is the title of David Niven's first volume of autobiography?

175 And the second?

176 What Bob Hope film was based on RUGGLES OF RED GAP?

177 What Hitchcock film was shot silent and hurriedly adapted for sound?

178 What famous film was adapted from Heinrich Mann's novel PROFESSOR UNRATH?

179 What comedian starred in THE STRONG MAN and TRAMP TRAMP TRAMP?

180 Who directed LA REGLE DU JEU?

181 Who played the two cricket enthusiasts in THE LADY VANISHES?

182 What Hitchcock film was based on a Francis Beeding novel, THE HOUSE OF DR EDWARDES?

183 Who starred in THE NEW YORK HAT, and who directed it?

184 Who created the Popeye cartoons?

185 Who played Irene, Sunny, Odette and Nell Gwyn?

186 Whose first sound film was SOUS LES TOITS DE PARIS?

187 Who directed THE DISCREET CHARM OF THE BOURGEOISIE?

188 What horror actor of the forties had fearsome features which were actually distorted by the disease acromegaly?

189 Who played Cantor Yoelson in THE JOLSON STORY?

190 In what film did Sig Rumann, Alexander Granach and Felix Bressart play as a team?

191 Of what film was Trudy Kockenlocker the heroine?

192 In what film was Cecil Kellaway stoppered in a bottle?

193 In what film was he gobbled up in a bathysphere?

194 Who photographed THE CAT AND THE CANARY (1939)?

195 Name the Chaplin comedy in which he polluted the waters of a health spa with alcohol.

196 Who played Captain Andy in the 1936 SHOWBOAT?

197 And in the 1951 remake?

198 What film from a play of the same name by Marc Connelly gave a simplistic Negro version of heaven and the Bible stories?

199 Who played De Lawd?

200 Who impersonated a gorilla in MY MAN GODFREY?

201 Who starred as CRAIG'S WIFE in 1936?

202 THE PETRIFIED FOREST was remade in 1946 as . . .

203 Who directed Garbo in CAMILLE?

204 Though Ruby Keeler's name was not used, who played her in THE JOLSON STORY?

205 What is the subject of CHAMPION, BODY AND SOUL and THE SET-UP?

206 When Leslie Howard was Romeo and Norma Shearer was Juliet, who was Mercutio?

207 Who won the Academy Award, in what film, for playing Mrs O'Leary?

208 What aerial melodrama won the first Academy Award as best film, in 1928?

209 For what film in which he repeated his stage role did Paul Lukas win an Oscar?

210 When NOTHING SACRED was remade, what was its new title, and who played Carole Lombard's role?

211 What role do Dame May Witty and Mona Washbourne have in common?

212 Who in 1938 played the title role in THE ADVENTURES OF TOM SAWYER?

213 Who directed METROPOLIS?

214 And who directed THE CABINET OF DR CALIGARI?

215 Who played Parris Mitchell in KINGS ROW?

216 Whose films include THUNDER BELOW, THE CHEAT and MY SIN?

217 Who directed THE SIGN OF THE CROSS?

218 What was added to the reissue during World War Two?

219 The first Mickey Mouse cartoon with sound had a watery setting. Name it.

220 What director began his Hollywood career by directing JOURNEY'S END, which he had directed on the London stage?

221 What was Marlene Dietrich's first American film?

222 Who played Gertrude to Olivier's HAMLET?

223 In what film did Astaire and Rogers perform the number MY ONE AND ONLY HIGHLAND FLING?

224 "No mean Machiavelli is smiling, cynical Sidney Kidd." Who played him in THE PHILADELPHIA STORY?

225 In BRINGING UP BABY, what kind of baby was it?

226 Who played the trumpet in GENEVIEVE?

227 Who directed DUCK SOUP?

228 Who played Dr Armstrong in the 1945 version of AND THEN THERE WERE NONE?

229 Who played Horace Femm in THE OLD DARK HOUSE and Dr Pretorious in THE BRIDE OF FRANKENSTEIN?

230 Who played Callahan in DESTRY RIDES AGAIN?

231 Who played the title role in MY GIRL TISA?

232　In that film, what politician saved the day, and who played him?

233　Who or what was LAUGHING GRAVY?

234　In what film was Inspector Cockrill the detective, and who played him?

235　What part did Charles Waldron play in THE BIG SLEEP?

236　Who played Magwitch in David Lean's GREAT EXPECTATIONS?

237　What comedian played two roles and spoofed himself in THANK YOUR LUCKY STARS?

238　Who were Charles Laughton's two leading ladies in REMBRANDT?

239　Who was BAMBI's rabbit friend?

240　Who wrote the novel BAMBI on which the film was based?

241　What segment of FANTASIA features crocodiles, ostriches and hippopotami?

242　Who directed ALL QUIET ON THE WESTERN FRONT?

243　Name the black acrobatic dancers who appeared mainly as speciality acts in Fox musicals of the forties.

244　Give the Christian names of the Ritz Brothers . . .

245　. . . and the Andrew Sisters.

246　Alan Ladd's last film was . . .

247　Who played Buckingham to Olivier's RICHARD III?

248　Who plays the title role in BARRY LYNDON?

249 What actor subsequently knighted made his first appearance in THE GHOUL?

250 Who played Scarlett O'Hara's mother in GONE WITH THE WIND?

251 "So they call me Concentration Camp Erhardt!" Name the film in which this line becomes a running gag.

252 Name the two leading players of INVASION OF THE BODY SNATCHERS.

THE OLD SCHOOLHOUSE DOOR (Easy)

In what film did each of the following play the leading role of a teacher?

1 Robert Donat

2 James Robertson Justice

3 Jane Wyman (TV movie)

4 Glenn Ford

5 Laurence Olivier

6 Margaret Rutherford

7 Jennifer Jones

8 Otto Kruger

9 Emil Jannings

10 Michael Redgrave

11 Bette Davis

12 Sidney Poitier

13 David Hemmings

14 Maggie Smith

15 Shirley MacLaine

16 Sandy Dennis

Poster 1. Name the missing film title.

1   Name the film in which Margaret O'Brien began her meteoric child star career as a London blitz orphan adopted by an American newspaperman.

2   Who played the title role in A GUY NAMED JOE?

3   Samuel Goldwyn in 1943 made a propaganda piece about a Russian village invaded by Nazis. When the cold war began it was an embarrassment and he sold off the rights; it later resurfaced, heavily cut, as ARMORED ATTACK. What was the original title?

4   Irene Dunne in 1944 made a film in which she married a landed Englishman, lost him in World War I and their son in World War II. Give the title.

5   The above film was based on a long narrative poem. By whom?

6   In 1944 MGM brought THE GOOD EARTH up to date by filming Pearl Buck's DRAGON SEED, about Chinese villagers at war. Who played Jade, the heroine?

7   In 1943 an eminent Broadway cast (including Ruth Gordon, Judith Anderson, Walter Huston and Morris Carnovsky) went to Hollywood and made a picture called EDGE OF DARKNESS, about Norwegian villagers resisting the Nazis. Who was the leading male star?

8   Cary Grant played the captain of a submarine in what 1943 adventure film? (The answer is *not* OPERATION PETTICOAT.)

9   Name the book by Jan Struther which was turned into Hollywood's most persuasive (if artificial) account of the British at war.

10   In 1941 Tyrone Power was A YANK IN THE RAF. Who was his leading lady?

11   Jules Dassin's first directorial chore, in 1942, concerned a loyal German American whose twin brother forced

him to aid the Nazis. Who played the dual role? What was the film?

12   In 1943 Howard Hawks made a film about the crew of a Flying Fortress called Mary Ann. Name it.

13   A book named EDUCATION FOR DEATH, by Gregor Ziemer, was the basis in 1943 of a surprisingly successful movie starring Bonita Granville and Kent Smith. Name it.

14   Jack L. Warner was later very sorry that in 1943 he produced a picture called MISSION TO MOSCOW, from Ambassador Joseph E. Davies' book promoting goodwill between Russia and America. Who played the ambassador?

15   Claudette Colbert, Paulette Goddard and Veronica Lake starred in 1943 as nurses trapped with the army on Corregidor. Name the picture.

16   Name also the very similar movie of the same year in which Margaret Sullavan, Joan Blondell and Ann Sothern played nurses caught on Bataan.

17   In FOUR JILLS IN A JEEP, an account of an actual USO tour by four stars, three of them were Carol Landis, Martha Raye and Mitzi Mayfair. Name the fourth.

18   Who played Colonel James Dolittle in THIRTY SECONDS OVER TOKYO?

19   In 1945 Errol Flynn appeared in a war movie which was banned in Britain because it ignored the British contribution in that particular theatre. Name it.

20   John Garfield played a blinded Marine named Al Schmid in a 1945 movie which began on Guadalcanal but became more of a documentary on help for returning veterans. Title, please.

BILLY THE KID (Medium)

William Bonney (1860–81) was a moronic juvenile delinquent who thought his gun made him a hero. He has not always been played this way in the movies. Can you say who appeared as Billy in the following films?

1 THE OUTLAW
2 DIRTY LITTLE BILLY
3 THE LEFT HANDED GUN
4 BILLY THE KID (1930)
5 BILLY THE KID (1940)
6 BILLY THE KID MEETS DRACULA
7 THE PARSON AND THE OUTLAW
8 THE LAW VERSUS BILLY THE KID
9 BILLY THE KID RETURNS
10 CHISUM

if you have

AILUROPHOBIA*

this picture could send you beyond the point of normal fear.

* deadly fear
of cats

Suggested for MATURE audiences
(parental discretion advised). Ⓜ

starring
Michael Sarrazin
Gayle Hunnicutt · Eleanor Parker co-starring Tim Henry

Music by LALO SCHIFRIN · Written by JOSEPH STEFANO · Directed by DAVID LOWELL RICH
Produced by BERNARD SCHWARTZ · A UNIVERSAL PICTURE in TECHNICOLOR®

Poster 2. Name the missing film title.

LADDERGRAMS

These puzzles produce lots of marks, so they're worth trying even though at first glance they may seem difficult.

The name by the arrow is the character name of a well-known star in a well-known movie. The real name of the actor can be read vertically down on the line of the arrow; one mark for getting that. Another mark for the name of the movie.

The horizontal lines which cross the name of the actor can be filled in with names of other performers with whom he or she has worked. In each case the clue on the right indicates the role of the latter in the film in question. One mark for the actor and one for the film.

For instance, if the name by the arrow were RICK BLAINE the vertical name would be HUMPHREY BOGART and the film would be CASABLANCA: two marks. The top horizontal line might read WALTER HUSTON, the H of HUMPHREY connecting with the H of HUSTON, in which case the clue might be PROSPECTOR and the film THE TREASURE OF THE SIERRA MADRE: one mark for Huston and one for the film.

It will be seen that it is not vital to complete the puzzle; just score as many marks as you can. Aim first, obviously, for the vertical name, which may materialise from allowing a mental picture to grow from a lazy perusal of all the clues at once.

No square is allowed for spaces between words: GRETA GARBO, for instance, would occupy ten spaces, and it is up to you to guess where the break comes. A few breaks and letters have however been filled in.

If the vertical name has twenty letters, the puzzle correctly completed will produce forty-two marks.

There are sixteen Laddergrams interspersed with the rest of the text.

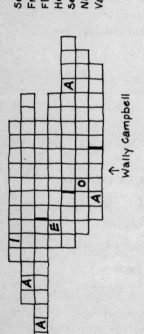

↑ Wally Campbell

Servant
Frightened heroine
Flyer
Health farm director
Servant
Nazi spy
Vaudevillian

Laddergram 1

31

THE WARNERS DO IT AGAIN (Difficult)

Warners was the studio most famous for economy in scripts: if a plot had once worked pretty well, they saw no reason not to use it again, and sometimes again and again, with a change of setting and/or a change of sex. Here are some Warner movies which were all made over from more famous originals. What originals?

1 SHE'S WORKING HER WAY THROUGH COLLEGE (1952)

2 THE STRAWBERRY BLONDE (1941)

3 LAW OF THE TROPICS (1941)

4 ILLEGAL (1955)

5 BARRICADE (1950)

6 SINCERELY YOURS (1955)

7 PAINTING THE CLOUDS WITH SUNSHINE (1951)

8 THEY MADE ME A CRIMINAL (1939)

9 TILL WE MEET AGAIN (1940)

10 YOUNG AT HEART (1955)

11 BETWEEN TWO WORLDS (1944)

12 HOUSE OF WOMEN (1962)

13 THE WAGONS ROLL AT NIGHT (1941)

14 CASTLE ON THE HUDSON (1940)

15 THAT WAY WITH WOMEN (1947)

16 SATAN MET A LADY (1936)

17 STOP YOU'RE KILLING ME (1952)

18 BRITISH INTELLIGENCE (1940)

19 COLORADO TERRITORY (1949)

20 ESCAPE IN THE DESERT (1945)

21 THE BREAKING POINT (1950)

22 THE UNFAITHFUL (1947)

23 INDIANAPOLIS SPEEDWAY (1939)

24 SINGAPORE WOMAN (1941)

25 TWO AGAINST THE WORLD (1936)

THE TELEHEROES (Easy)

A surname is often a sufficient label for a TV series which runs for several seasons, and it usually indicates tough action. Can you name the actors who brought the following he-men into your living-room?

1 BRONCO

2 MANNIX

3 MAVERICK (there were three)

4 CANNON

5 DELVECCHIO

6 SHANNON

7 CALLAN

8 SERPICO

9 HAWK

10 IRONSIDE

11 McCLOUD

12 BANACEK

13 DANTE

14 STACCATO

15 MARKHAM

The following gave their full names. Does that make it easier?

16 RICHARD DIAMOND

17 MICHAEL SHAYNE

18 PHILIP MARLOWE

19 DAN RAVEN

20 BAT MASTERSON

21 PETER GUNN

22 CHINA SMITH

23 STONEY BURKE

24 JOE FORRESTER

A CINEGUILD PRODUCTION · A PRODUCT OF THE J. ARTHUR RANK ORGANISATION

Poster 3. Name the missing film title.

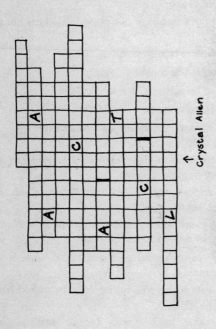

Flyer
Ex-husband
Killer
Plastic surgeon
Western lady
Violinist
Walker
Ice skater
Lover victim
Poetic postman
Friend
Blind pianist

↑ Crystal Allen

Laddergram 2

37

IN TWO WORDS, IM POSSIBLE (Medium)

In what films did the following unlikely events take place?

1   Irene Dunne found a natural supply of money in the garden. (1952)

2   A caterpillar danced to the strains of Yes, Sir, That's My Baby. (1944)

3   An angel gave a downtrodden, despairing hero a review of his past life. (1945)

4   A murdered girl came back as a ghost to trap her killer. (1941)

5   A baby was able to talk like an adult. (1960)

6   A man discovered he could fly. (1966)

7   A cat avenged her mistress' murder. (1962)

8   The voice of God spoke on the radio. (1950)

9   A Model T Ford was driven through the air over Washington. (1961)

10 Baseballs were made of a special material enabling them to curve away from the batsmen. (1950)

11 A dog was reincarnated as Dick Powell and solved his own murder. (1950)

12 Scientists were miniaturised and injected into the blood stream of a scientist to save his life. (1967)

13 A pixillated toucan spread good feelings through New York City. (1968)

14 A timid soul found his true metier when he turned into a dolphin. (1964)

15 An atomic cloud made a man become smaller and smaller until he was invisible to the naked eye. (1957)

16 A cat became the owner of a baseball team. (1950)

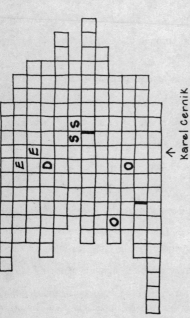

Karel Cernik

Frivolous lady
Defence counsel
Warlock
Wife
Escaped convict
Writer's wife
Queen
Shady lady
Playwright's wife
Employee
General
Pursuing policeman

Laddergram 3

39

ALFRED HITCHCOCK PRESENTS (Easy)

What Hitchcock film:

1 Was based on the true case of Manny Balestrero?

2 Was written by Raymond Chandler and Czenzi Ormonde?

3 Had a famous single shot which began by taking in an entire dance hall and ended up focusing on the twitching eye of the drummer?

4 Featured Wylie Watson as Mr Memory?

5 Was shot in Munich, San Remo and Lake Como?

6 Had a shot up through the ceiling showing pacing feet in the room above?

7 Was a whodunit starring Herbert Marshall?

8 Had John Gavin as hero?

9 Was photographed entirely in one set? (Two answers.)

10 Had Albert Bassermann as Van Meer?

11 Was based on a book by Somerset Maugham?

12 Was based on a book by Joseph Conrad?

13 Concerned a fisherman and a lawyer in love with the same girl?

14 Included a sequence in Radio City Music Hall?

15 Climaxed with a chase through the British Museum?

16 Had a scene in which the hero outwitted a villainous dentist and forced him to inhale his own chloroform?

17 Featured Jessie Royce Landis as the hero's mother?

18 Allowed the director to make his usual quick appearance only as a reducing ad in a newspaper?

19 Had the villain, by use of subjective camera, shoot himself and the audience at the same time?

20 Had a scene in which the heroine found a shrunken head in her bed?

Poster 4. Name the missing film title.

OSCAR, I LOVE YOU (Easy)

For what films did the following actors and actresses receive Academy Awards?

1   Gale Sondergaard

2   Thomas Mitchell

3   Bing Crosby

4   Bette Davis (2)

5   Ronald Colman

6   Walter Brennan (3)

7   Helen Hayes (2)

8   Marie Dressler

9   Paul Lukas

10   Ginger Rogers

11   Joan Fontaine

12   James Cagney

13   Katharine Hepburn (3, including one shared)

And for what films did the following directors receive them?

14   Frank Lloyd (2)

15   Leo McCarey (3)

16   Norman Taurog

17   Michael Curtiz

SILENCE PLEASE I (Medium)

1 In 1925 John Barrymore appeared in THE SEA BEAST. From what classic novel was this adapted?

2 In 1921 Charles Chaplin discovered and trained a new child star for his film THE KID. Who was he?

3 In 1922 Alan Crosland directed the first film with talking sequences. What was it?

4 What film released in 1916 was originally intended to be called THE MOTHER AND THE LAW?

5 THE MIRACLE MAN in 1919 included a part requiring a contortionist rather than an actor. The man who played it rapidly became a star. Who was he?

6 In 1919–20 Cecil B. De Mille made three society dramas (FOR BETTER FOR WORSE, DON'T CHANGE YOUR HUSBAND, MALE AND FEMALE) with the same leading lady. Name her.

7 A big box-office hit of 1925 was STELLA DALLAS, later remade as a talkie with Barbara Stanwyck. Who played the title role in the silent film?

8 Who played "the chink" in BROKEN BLOSSOMS in 1919?

9 In Britain for about ten years from 1917, big commercial successes were society dramas featuring a husband-and-wife team. She was Ivy Duke. Who was he?

10 Also in Britain, name the music hall comedian who made popular screen comedies in the twenties, including PREHISTORIC MAN.

11 Name the Broadway stage actress who in 1918–19 was appearing in such films as OUR MISS McCHESNEY and THE DIVORCE, made only one film in the next twenty-five years, but became a Hollywood star again in old age.

12 Who came to fame as THE LONE WOLF in 1917?

13 Whose 1922 starring vehicles included BEYOND THE ROCKS and MORAN OF THE LADY LETTY?

14 In 1923 Harold Lloyd made his first skyscraper-climbing comedy. Name it.

15 What celebrated (and lengthy) film of 1923 starred Zasu Pitts, Gibson Gowland and Jean Hersholt?

16 Who directed it?

17 In 1926–27 a famous team came together in films including PUTTING PANTS ON PHILIP, LOVE 'EM AND WEEP and DO DETECTIVES THINK? Who were they?

18 In what 1924 film did Lon Chaney play a circus clown?

19 In 1913 Cecil B. De Mille made his first film in Hollywood. It is also claimed as the first film made in Hollywood by anybody. What was it?

20 In 1919 THE CABINET OF DR CALIGARI starred as the somnambulist a German actor who in the thirties and forties became a popular hero/villain of English speaking films. Who was he?

COPYCATS: FIRST DIVISION (Difficult)

What, in terms of roles they have played, do the following actors have in common? Name the films concerned.

1 Cary Grant, Clifton Webb, Claude Rains

2 Cary Grant, Jack Lemmon, Jimmy Durante

3 Ronald Colman, Jack Benny, Richard Burton

4 Barry K. Barnes, Leslie Howard, David Niven

5 Keefe Brasselle, Larry Parks, Barbra Streisand

6 John Barrymore, Fredric March, Spencer Tracy

7 Irene Dunne, Anna Neagle, Fay Compton

8 Clifton Webb, Richard Chamberlain, Maurice Evans, Wilfred Lawson

9 Anna Neagle, Burt Lancaster, Betty Hutton, Groucho Marx

10 John Gielgud, George Arliss, Alec Guinness

11 Cecil Kellaway, Jimmy O'Dea, Tommy Steele, Don Beddoe

12 Michael Rennie, Jeff Morrow, James Arness, Paul Birch

13 Arthur Franz, Jon Hall, Vincent Price

14 Phyllis Calvert, Joanne Woodward, Eleanor Parker

15 Henry Fonda, Lew Ayres, Fredric March, Peter Sellers

16 Humphrey Bogart, Ronald Colman, Steve McQueen, Joseph Schildkraut

17   Allison Hayes, Buddy Baer, Glenn Langan

18   Ray Milland, Walter Huston, Laird Cregar

19   Judy Garland, Albert Finney, David Niven

20   Cedric Hardwicke, Maria Casares, Fredric March

21   Yul Brynner, Jean Peters, Robert Newton

22   Yvonne de Carlo, Doris Day, Jean Arthur

23   Erich von Stroheim, Danny Kaye, Michael Redgrave

24   Montagu Love, Charles Laughton, Sid James

25   Nancy Coleman, Ida Lupino, Olivia de Havilland

26   James Garner, Burt Lancaster, Henry Fonda

27   Bobby Watson, Luther Adler, Richard Basehart

28   Boris Karloff, Warner Oland, Peter Lorre

29   Kay Hammond, Robert Donat, Rex Harrison

30   Lee Remick, Gig Young, Ray Milland

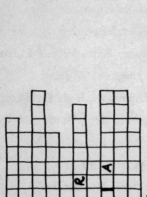

Patriot
Usurper
Pirate
Queen
Actress
C.O.s wife
Henry VIII
Villain
Nazi
Dancer

Kerry Bradford

Laddergram 4

48

Poster 5. Name the missing film title.

IT STARTED THIS WAY (Easy)

What well-known films began with these scenes?

1   A married woman dreams of a deserted and derelict manor-house.

2   Baskul is evacuated.

3   A high wire fence bears a notice: NO TRESPASSING.

4   A fat man listens to a scratchy gramophone in a room in Istanbul.

5   A man in a dark suit walks along a paved highway and stops outside a truckdrivers' cafe.

6   A man tampers with a clock at a lunch wagon counter.

7   A fort full of dead men is found in the Sahara.

8   A dock worker sings to himself as he strolls along just before six a.m.

9   A barrage of shots and miscellaneous noises leads the eye to a sign reading WELCOME TO BOTTLENECK.

10 A Venetian gondolier fills his craft full of garbage and glides away singing a barcarolle.

11 A man walks out on his wife. Following him to the door, she smilingly breaks one of his golf clubs. About to strike her, he thinks better of it and pushes her to the ground.

12 While a private eye waits to be announced, the daughter of the house falls into his arms.

13 At a one-horse desert town, a one-armed stranger gets off the train.

14 An aged actor speaks at an awards dinner.

15 Having driven recklessly through the night streets, a
man lets himself into an empty office building and
begins to speak into a dictaphone.

16 A gossip columnist interviews stars arriving at a Hollywood premiere many years ago.

17 A train pulls into Vienna's railway station.

18 Three Russians inspect the foyer of an expensive Paris
hotel.

19 A diner in a restaurant finds that the lady he invited
has been sitting with her back to him at the next table.

20 A gentleman recently deceased descends to the shades
and presents his credentials to His Excellency.

21 An unsuccessful young man visits his father in a nudist
camp.

22 A doctor returns to his small town and finds that his
friends, acquaintances and patients are not quite themselves.

23 A heavily-bandaged gentleman arrives at an English
inn.

24 A ship is torpedoed, and survivors clinging to a life
raft relive their recent lives.

25 A film producer, off on a voyage of exploration, picks
up the girl who is to be his heroine in a waterfront cafe.

TUT, TUT (Easy)

Some questions about films which in their time extended the bounds of permissiveness.

1 Who starred in OUR DANCING DAUGHTERS, OUR MODERN MAIDENS and OUR BLUSHING BRIDES?

2 What Otto Preminger comedy was issued in defiance of the Production Code ban?

3 Clark Gable as Rhett Butler in GONE WITH THE WIND was finally allowed to speak a line which offended the Hays Office. What was it?

4 Who rewrote Noël Coward's DESIGN FOR LIVING for the screen, leaving, he believed, just one of the Master's lines?

5 What much-banned novel, by whom, was filmed in 1933 as THE STORY OF TEMPLE DRAKE?

6 Who sang, in what film, I LIKE A MAN WHO TAKES HIS TIME?

7 Who wrote the play WHO'S AFRAID OF VIRGINIA WOOLF?

8 What was missing from the version of THE BACHELOR PARTY released in Great Britain?

9 Name the three leading actresses in THE KILLING OF SISTER GEORGE.

10 In what film did Hedy Lamarr swim in the nude, and who directed it?

11   By the time MY FAIR LADY was made, the phrase
     "not bloody likely" which had caused such a commotion
     in the original PYGMALION, was felt to be too tame.
     What phrase – applied to a horse at Ascot – replaced it?

12   What 1945 British film had to be reshot because the ladies'
     decolletage was too revealing for American audiences?

13   And why did the Americans reject David Lean's
     OLIVER TWIST?

14   In what film did Mickey Shaughnessy mouth obsceni-
     ties which the sound track obligingly bleeped out?

15   In what film did Rex Harrison instruct a lady to "piss
     off"?

FLASHBACK (Easy)

It used to be fashionable to tell stories in retrospect. Name the films which had their stories narrated by:

1   A dead man floating in a pool.

2   Humphrey Bogart, to a priest.

3   Brian Donlevy, while tending bar.

4   Charles Boyer, to Mitchell Leisen.

5   Elsa Lanchester, to actors playing two famous poets.

6   Joan Fontaine, as a character with no first name.

7   Herbert Marshall, as a famous author.

8   A house.

9   Alec Guinness, in South America.

10   George Montgomery, to a barman.

11   Robert Benchley, mostly in insets.

12   Spencer Tracy, straight to camera.

13   Marlon Brando, straight to camera.

14   Denis Price, via his character's memoirs.

15   Flora Robson, to Miles Mander.

Second lead
Gypsy
Rich man
Investigator
Chess player
Nervous hero
Scientist
Bird-man
Gangster
Stranded guest
Opera singer
Newspaper publisher

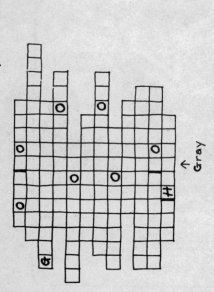

Gray

Laddergram 5

Poster 6. Name the missing film title.

THEY WENT TO THE MOVIES (Medium)

In what film did:

1 Doris Day go to the movies and watch herself?

2 Larry Parks do likewise?

3 Dorothy McGuire watch a silent movie?

4 Louis Jourdan take Linda Christian to see SON OF THE SHEIK?

5 Astronauts in orbit watch Rosemary Clooney in HERE COME THE GIRLS?

6 Convicts see THE EGG AND I?

7 Sailors watch THE WALKING DEAD (disguised as YOUNG DR JEKYLL MEETS FRANKENSTEIN)?

8 Convicts roar with laughter at a Disney cartoon?

9 Convicts see WINGS OF THE NAVY?

10 A small town audience watch RED RIVER?

11 Peter Sellers project COMING THRO' THE RYE?

12 Gloria Swanson watch herself in QUEEN KELLY?

THEY SUFFERED A SEA CHANGE I (Medium)

Many American films have their titles changed in Britain, for reasons good and bad. B F's DAUGHTER, for instance, could hardly be used in Britain, where a B F is a bloody fool, so it become POLLY FULTON. But why AN AMERICAN DREAM should become SEE YOU IN HELL DARLING is anybody's guess, apart from the fact that the mention of America in a title is supposed to be a jinx in Britain. Here are some changed titles of American films as they appeared in Britain: see if you can work out the original titles. The main star is given to help you.

1 BIG DEAL AT DODGE CITY (1966) Henry Fonda

2 THE MOVING TARGET (1966) Paul Newman

3 WHAT A MAN (1941) W. C. Fields

4 ESCAPE TO HAPPINESS (1940) Leslie Howard

5 THE MURDER IN THORNTON SQUARE (1944) Charles Boyer

6 ONE BORN EVERY MINUTE (1967) George C. Scott

7 THE ANATOLIAN SMILE (1963) Stathis Giallelis

8 STRICTLY CONFIDENTIAL (1935) Warner Baxter

9 UNCONVENTIONAL LINDA (1938) Cary Grant

10 BACHELOR GIRL APARTMENT (1967) Jane Fonda

11 BACHELOR KNIGHT (1947) Cary Grant

12 MURDER INC. (1951) Humphrey Bogart

13 ONE MAN MUTINY (1956) Gary Cooper

14 THE MAGNIFICENT SHOWMAN (1964) John Wayne

15 THE GRIP OF FEAR (1962) Glenn Ford

16 PRECINCT 45 – LOS ANGELES POLICE (1971) George C. Scott

17 DYNAMITE MAN FROM GLORY JAIL (1973) James Stewart

18 THE WORLD AND HIS WIFE (1948) Spencer Tracy

19 BUILD MY GALLOWS HIGH (1948) Robert Mitchum

20 MAN AND HIS MATE (1939) Victor Mature

UP TO DATE (Easy)

For the very young film buffs who don't watch television, here are some questions on the films of 1975 and 1976.

1   What studio made THE DAY OF THE LOCUST?

2   Who wrote, produced and directed AT LONG LAST LOVE?

3   Who directed LUCKY LADY?

4   What famous night club owner, impresario and composer was played by James Caan in FUNNY LADY?

5   Who wrote the novel JAWS?

6   Who played LEPKE?

7   Glenda Jackson and Susannah York appeared in a film the title of which explained their roles. Name it.

8   What was to be feared in PHASE IV?

9   Who directed PHASE IV, and for what is he better known?

10   Who played the wife of THE PRISONER OF SECOND AVENUE?

11   Who produced, directed and co-wrote THE RETURN OF THE PINK PANTHER?

12   Who wrote CHINATOWN and co-wrote SHAMPOO?

13   What historical character was played by Brian Keith in THE WIND AND THE LION?

14   The writer-producer-director of DOC SAVAGE was first famous for films of what kind? Name him.

15 Who played Claire Trevor's old part in FAREWELL MY LOVELY?

16 In what city did FRENCH CONNECTION NUMBER TWO take place?

17 Name the Tennessee sheriff about whom WALKING TALL and its sequel were made.

18 In what city was RUSSIAN ROULETTE set?

19 Who played the assassin Joubert in THREE DAYS OF THE CONDOR?

20 Name the novel on which THREE DAYS OF THE CONDOR was based.

21 Name the film starring Burt Reynolds, directed by John Avildsen, set in 1957 and telling of a touring band. (Get it *right*!)

22 Who played Sherlock Holmes and Dr Watson in THE ADVENTURE OF SHERLOCK HOLMES' SMARTER BROTHER?

23 Who photographed BARRY LYNDON?

24 The roles of Effie and Wilmer in THE MALTESE FALCON were reprised 35 years later by the same actors in THE BLACK BIRD. Name the actors.

25 Name the sequel to HARPER, starring Paul Newman.

Poster 7. Name the missing film title.

Son
Holiday aquaintance
Husband
Soldier
Cowboy
Ex-husband
Future son-in-law
Composer
Producer
Father
Reporter
Skipper
Flyer
Teacher
Industrialist husband
Politician

↑ Linda Seton

Laddergram 6

63

REMAKE ROLES (Easy)

Each pair of actors played the same key role in different versions of the same story. Give the title(s) and the roles.

1 Pauline Lord, Fay Bainter

2 Basil Rathbone, John Hodiak

3 Maria Ouspenskaya, Cathleen Nesbitt

4 Fay Wray, Phyllis Kirk

5 Ginger Rogers, Debbie Reynolds

6 John Barrymore, Adolphe Menjou

7 Aline McMahon, Ethel Barrymore

8 Leslie Howard, Tyrone Power

9 Leslie Howard, David Niven

10 Bette Davis, Susan Hayward

11 Marlene Dietrich, Brigitte Bardot

12 Rudolph Valentino, Bob Hope

13 Pat O'Brien, Rosalind Russell

14 Carole Lombard, Jerry Lewis

15 Ginger Rogers, Jerry Lewis

16 Charles Laughton, Bob Hope

17 Charles Ruggles, Jack Benny

18 H. B. Warner, John Gielgud

19 Lionel Stander, Jack Carson

20 Paul Muni, Kay Francis

21 Clark Gable, Jack Lemmon

22 Edna Best, Doris Day

23 Sam Jaffe, Sammy Davis Jnr

24 Oliver Hardy, Jack Haley

25 Shirley Booth, Barbra Streisand

26 Charles Coburn, Cary Grant

27 Wendy Hiller, Audrey Hepburn

28 Theda Bara, Claudette Colbert

29 W. C. Fields, Ralph Richardson

30 Edward Van Sloan, Peter Cushing

THE VERY MAN (Easy)

Name the actor who played each of the following title roles.

1 A MAN FOR ALL SEASONS

2 THE MAN (TV movie)

3 THE INVISIBLE MAN (1933)

4 THE INDESTRUCTIBLE MAN

5 THE MAN IN GREY

6 THE MAN IN HALF MOON STREET

7 THE MAN FROM LARAMIE

8 THE MAN FROM THE ALAMO

9 A MAN ALONE

10 MAN ABOUT TOWN

11 A MAN AND A WOMAN

12 THE MAN I MARRIED

13 THE MAN IN THE WHITE SUIT

14 THE MAN IN THE GREY FLANNEL SUIT

15 MAN OF A THOUSAND FACES

16 THE FLIM FLAM MAN

17 THE MAN WITHOUT A STAR

18 THE MAN WITHOUT A COUNTRY (TV movie)

19 THE MAN WHO CRIED WOLF

20 THE MAN WITH THE GOLDEN ARM

21 THE MAN WHO BROKE THE BANK AT MONTE CARLO

22 THE MAN WHO CAME TO DINNER

23 THE THIN MAN (think twice)

24 THE MAN WHO RECLAIMED HIS HEAD

25 THE MAN WHO PLAYED GOD

26 A MAN TO REMEMBER

27 THE MAN WHO COULD CHEAT DEATH

28 THE MAN WHO UNDERSTOOD WOMEN

29 THE MAN WHO LOVED CAT DANCING

30 THE MAN WHO SHOT LIBERTY VALANCE

NO SUB-TITLES REQUIRED (Medium)

Foreign language films have sometimes been so successful in their own countries that Hollywood or British studios have bought up the rights and made English language versions, usually poorer than the originals, and often at the cost of the loss of those originals to the public. Can you name the English language remakes of the following? Also the star who replaced the one shown below?

1   LE JOUR SE LEVE (France, 1939, Jean Gabin)

2   PIEGES (France, 1939, Maurice Chevalier)

3   RASHOMON (Japan, 1950, Toshiro Mifune)

4   LE BETE HUMAINE (France, 1938, Jean Gabin)

5   MONSIEUR LA SOURIS (France, 1942, Raimu)

6   LA MORT DU CYGNE (France, 1937, Mia Slavenska (adult role))

7   THE HANDS OF ORLAC (German, 1926, Conrad Veidt)

8   PEPE LE MOKO (France, 1937, Jean Gabin)

9   LES INCONNUS DANS LA MAISON (France, 1942, Raimu)

10   YOJIMBO (Japan, 1961, Toshiro Mifune) (actually remade in Italy)

11   LE CORBEAU (France, 1943, Pierre Fresnay)

12   SEVEN SAMURAI (Japan, 1954, Toshiro Mifune)

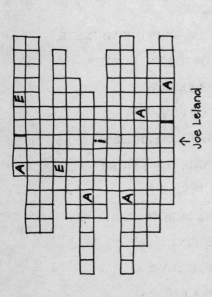

Former U-boat commander
Older brother
Captain Trumbull
Hood
Rich girl
Sergeant
Younger brother
Sergeant
Nurse
South Sea priest
Cripple
Singer

↑ Joe Leland

NB In this puzzle, one actor appears twice

Laddergram 7

69

WHAT'S IN A NAME? (Medium)

The title of a film is frequently changed during production. Give the titles under which the following were eventually released.

1 EIGHT ARMS TO HOLD YOU

2 MY LAST DUCHESS

3 THE CENTURIONS

4 LADY KILLER/A COMEDY OF MURDERS

5 THE LONELY STAGE

6 CHUCK-A-LUCK

7 DARLING, I AM GROWING YOUNGER

8 THE VOICE OF HELEN McCORD

9 ANYONE FOR VENICE?

10 THE STORY OF FIVE WIVES

11 NOT TONIGHT, JOSEPHINE

12 THE LADY AND THE KNIGHT

13 MOTHER SUPERIOR

14 KING OF THE MOUNTAIN

15 SOBBIN' WOMEN

16 WE BELIEVE IN LOVE

17 TRIBUTE TO A BAD MAN

18 I LOVE LOUISA (3 possible answers)

19 BATS WITH BABY FACES

20 THE INNOCENT

21 FEMALE OF THE SPECIES

22 THE RICHMOND STORY

23 THE PARACHUTISTS ARE COMING

24 NOBODY LOVES A DRUNKEN INDIAN

WHEN DISASTER STRUCK (Easy)

1   Name the star who played Lady Edwina Esketh in THE
    RAINS CAME, the name of the actress in the remake,
    the title of that remake, and the author of the original
    novel.

2   Who played the Iron Jaw Woman in what Cecil B. De
    Mille epic which climaxed in a train wreck?

3   What athletic hero began his career in 1938 in THE
    HURRICANE, and what 'monster' did he later portray?

4   In what silent epic was the fall of Babylon depicted, and
    who directed it?

5   Disaster was narrowly averted in a film in which Helen
    Hayes played a stowaway. Name the film and the author
    of the original novel.

6   A British film about a famous disaster featured Kenneth
    More, Honor Blackman, Michael Goodliffe and David
    McCallum. Name the film and the year of the disaster.

7   What kind of disaster is common to THE BLUE BIRD
    (1940) and BAMBI? Name the original author in each
    case.

8   What disaster movie had a geographically incorrect title?

9   Which historical character, allegedly responsible for
    starting a celebrated disaster, has been played by Peter
    Lorre, Peter Ustinov, and Charles Laughton; and in
    what films?

10 What disaster film of the seventies was directed by
    Ronald Neame from a novel by Paul Gallico?

11 In what film was Bette Davis caught up in the San
    Francisco earthquake of 1906? Who wrote the original
    novel?

12   In what film did Rod Taylor play a pilot whose apparent error caused a disaster on take-off which was investigated by Glenn Ford? Who wrote the original novel?

13   Name the film in which Linda Darnell fled from the London fire of 1666. Name the author of the original novel.

14   In THE GOOD EARTH, Chinese life and livelihood were threatened by a plague of . . . what? Who wrote the original novel?

15   What kind of disaster was common to THE BRAVE DON'T CRY, THE PROUD VALLEY and BLACK FURY?

16   In which film were John Mills and Richard Attenborough trapped in a submarine at the bottom of the sea?

17   What natural phenomenon threatened the cast of THE DEVIL AT FOUR O'CLOCK? Who wrote the original novel?

18   Name the science fiction producer responsible for, among others, THE WAR OF THE WORLDS, CONQUEST OF SPACE and WHEN WORLDS COLLIDE.

19   Who was the author of THINGS TO COME? What did he prophesy for 1940? What followed it?

20   What natural disaster was common to THE LAST DAYS OF POMPEII and HER JUNGLE LOVE?

Poster 8. Name the missing film title.

BIG JOHN (Easy)

In what film did John Wayne:

1 Consult a doctor played by James Stewart?

2 Play Captain Nathan Brittles?

3 Have Oliver Hardy as a follower?

4 Antagonise Red Will Danaher?

5 Co-star with Lauren Bacall?

6 Play Genghis Khan?

7 Fall for a Russian aviatrix?

8 Build a railroad in the Andes?

9 Succumb to a giant squid?

10 Play a centurion?

11 Have Earl Holliman and Michael Anderson for brothers?

12 Romance Elsa Martinelli?

13 Lead a party of settlers to Oregon?

14 Have the berth below Claudette Colbert?

15 Chase communists in Hawaii?

16 Get stranded in Labrador?

FROM THE ORIGINAL PLAY (Medium)

Name the films made from these plays.

1   BIRTHDAY by Laszlo Bus-Fekete

2   HEAVEN CAN WAIT by Harry Segall

3   MATILDA SHOUTED FIRE by Janet Green

4   YEARS AGO by Ruth Gordon

5   WASHINGTON SQUARE by Henry James

6   THE MERCHANT OF YONKERS by Thornton Wilder

7   DIAMOND LIL by Mae West

8   EVERYBODY COMES TO RICK'S by Murray Burnett and Joan Alison

9   LILIOM by Ferenc Molnar

10 NAPOLEON OF BROADWAY by Charles Bruce Milholland

11 THE TIME OF THE CUCKOO by Arthur Laurents

12 THE MILK TRAIN DOESN'T STOP HERE ANY MORE by Tennessee Williams

13 AMY JOLLY by Benno Vigny

14 THE SILENT VOICE by Jules Eckert Goodman

15 THE TEMPEST by William Shakespeare

16 THE SLEEPING PRINCESS by Terence Rattigan

17 DR PRAETORIOUS by Curt Goetz

18 COME PRIMO MELLIO DE PRIMA by Luigi Pirandello

19 HENRY IV, PARTS ONE AND TWO, by William Shakespeare

20 FRAGILE FOX by Norman Brooks

21 CUISINE DES ANGES by Albert Husson

22 A LOSS OF ROSES by William Inge

23 GREEN GROW THE LILACS by Lynn Riggs

24 JOAN OF LORRAINE by Maxwell Anderson

DUCHESS OF HOLLYWOOD (Easy)

In what film did Bette Davis:

1 Wear jodhpurs and drink poison?

2 Play Billie Burke's daughter?

3 Play Queen Elizabeth I for the second time?

4 Scandalise her family by wearing a red dress?

5 Watch an execution with George Brent?

6 Go mad in court?

7 Get murdered? (Two answers)

8 Play a bedridden invalid?

9 Cover a small-town wedding?

10 Play twins? (Two answers)

11 Console Claude Rains?

12 Murder Claude Rains?

13 Wear only the top half of her pyjamas?

14 Kill her lover?

15 Allow her husband to die?

16 Go mad and run away into the darkness?

A GOOD CAST IS WORTH REPEATING (Medium)

So ran the announcement at the end of old Universal movies. But can you name the films which featured these groups of actors? They are not necessarily in order of billing, and the nominal star is not always included.

1. Lee Marvin, Anne Bancroft, Raymond Burr, Lee J. Cobb
2. Lee Marvin, Ernest Borgnine, Dean Jagger, Spencer Tracy
3. Lee J. Cobb, George Voskovec, Jack Warden, Ed Begley
4. Onslow Stevens, Lionel Atwill, Lon Chaney Jnr, John Carradine
5. Ernest Thesiger, Eva Moore, Gloria Stuart, Charles Laughton
6. Thomas Mitchell, Jane Darwell, Harry Davenport, Leslie Howard
7. Gladys Cooper, Nigel Bruce, Reginald Denny, Joan Fontaine
8. Everett Sloane, Joseph Cotten, Gus Schilling, George Coulouris
9. George Zucco, Gale Sondergaard, John Beal, Bob Hope
10. Josephine Hull, Jean Adair, Peter Lorre, Cary Grant
11. Frank Morgan, Billie Burke, Bert Lahr, Jack Haley
12. Melvyn Douglas, Ina Claire, Felix Bressart, Sig Ruman
13. Frank Sinatra, Gene Kelly, Jules Munshin, Esther Williams
14. Peter Lorre, Boris Karloff, Bela Lugosi, Kay Kyser
15. Frank Reicher, Fay Wray, Robert Armstrong, Bruce Cabot
16. John Wayne, Frank Sinatra, Yul Brynner, Senta Berger

17 Richard Conte, James Caan, Diane Keaton, Sterling Hayden

18 Robert Shaw, Wendy Hiller, Susannah York, Orson Welles

19 George Kennedy, Barbara Hale, Dean Martin, Jean Seberg

20 James Stewart, Ruth Hussey, Roland Young, Virginia Weidler

21 Barry Fitzgerald, Victor McLaglen, Maureen O'Hara, John Wayne

22 Dame May Whitty, Paul Lukas, Michael Redgrave, Cecil Parker

23 Eve Arden, Arthur O'Connell, Ben Gazzara, Lee Remick

24 Ava Gardner, Martin Balsam, Burt Lancaster, Fredric March

25 Carroll Baker, Mercedes McCambridge, Elizabeth Taylor

26 Marilyn Monroe, Hugh Marlowe, Gregory Ratoff, George Sanders

27 John McIntyre, Vera Miles, Martin Balsam, John Gavin

28 Myrna Loy, Teresa Wright, Hoagy Carmichael, Dana Andrews

29 Martha Raye, Jane Frazee, Hugh Herbert, Mischa Auer

30 Bette Davis, Claude Rains, Brian Aherne, John Garfield

31 Thomas Mitchell, Jean Arthur, Guy Kibbee, Claude Rains

32 Myrna Loy, George Brent, Maria Ouspenskaya, Nigel Bruce

33 Bela Lugosi, Maria Ouspenskaya, Warren William, Claude Rains

34 Maria Ouspenskaya, Claude Rains, Charles Coburn, Nancy Coleman

35 John Howard, Jane Wyatt, Edward Everett Horton, H. B. Warner

36 Claude Rains, Basil Rathbone, Ian Hunter, Olivia de Havilland

37 Claude Rains, Henry Daniell, Flora Robson, Brenda Marshall

38 Lee J. Cobb, Vincent Price, William Eythe, Charles Bickford

39 Vincent Price, Cedric Hardwicke, Nan Grey, John Sutton

40 Vincent Price, Basil Rathbone, Boris Karloff, Barbara O'Neil

41 Vincent Price, Peter Lorre, Boris Karloff, Jack Nicholson

42 Vincent Price, Cedric Hardwicke, William Eythe, Alexander Knox

43 Gene Tierney, Don Ameche, Laird Cregar, Eugene Pallette

44 Claude Rains, Edward Everett Horton, Evelyn Keyes, Halliwell Hobbes

45 David Frost, Maggie Smith, Rod Taylor, Louis Jourdan

46 Al Jolson, Hobart Cavanagh, Tyrone Power, Alice Faye

47 Bette Davis, Claude Rains, Paul Henried, Gladys Cooper

48 Bette Davis, Claude Rains, Walter Abel, Jerome Cowan

49 Humphrey Bogart, Mary Astor, Sidney Greenstreet, Sen Yung

50 Humphrey Bogart, Sidney Greenstreet, Peter Lorre, S. Z. Sakall

BLESS THESE HOUSES (Easy)

The answers are films with the word HOUSE in the title. Name the house:

1 In which Lon Chaney Jnr was cured of lycanthropy.

2 In which Shelley Winters played a famous madam.

3 Which changed insects to birds and starred Robert Taylor.

4 Introduced Emergo and included in its cast Carol Ohmart and Elisha Cook Jnr.

5 Which, as a TV pilot film, starred Christopher George, but led to a series starring Burt Reynolds.

6 In which Vincent Price played a role first essayed by Lionel Atwill.

7 Which used the March of Time technique to uncover communist spies.

8 Which had its plot reused by BROKEN LANCE and THE BIG SHOW.

9 In which Robert Ryan ran rackets in Tokyo.

10 In which Orson Welles was cornered on the Colosseum in Rome.

War correspondent
Indian
Railroad magnate
D.A.
Botany professor
Law enforcer
Possible spouse
Clay Dalzell
Juror
Shell-shocked war veteran
War correspondent
Psychiatrist

Dale Tremont

Laddergram 8

83

THE ADVENTURES OF . . . WHO? (Easy)

All the following films are episodes from series featuring a continuing character. Name the series.

1 SHADOWS IN THE NIGHT

2 THE BISHOP MURDER CASE

3 MURDER OVER NEW YORK

4 DIG THAT URANIUM

5 BLUE WHITE AND PERFECT

6 THE AMBUSHERS

7 JUNGLE MOON MEN

8 ONE DANGEROUS NIGHT

9 FOOTLIGHT GLAMOUR

10 THE HILLS OF HOME

11 DARK DELUSION

12 RIDE ON VAQUERO

13 A FAMILY AFFAIR

14 PURSUIT TO ALGIERS

15 THE PHANTOM PLAINSMEN

16 REMEDY FOR RICHES

17 FOLLOW THAT CAMEL

18 THE FATAL HOUR

19 YOU ONLY LIVE TWICE

20 13 LEAD SOLDIERS

MATCHED PAIRS (Medium)

Who played:

1   THE BARONESS AND THE BUTLER in 1937?

2   HER HIGHNESS AND THE BELLBOY in 1945?

3   THUNDERBOLT AND LIGHTFOOT in 1974?

4   THE FEMINIST AND THE FUZZ (TV movie) in 1971?

5   TARZAN AND THE LEOPARD WOMAN in 1946?

6   THE PRIZEFIGHTER AND THE LADY in 1933?

7   CAIN AND MABEL in 1936?

8   THE BABBITT AND THE BROMIDE, (in ZIEGFELD FOLLIES) in 1946?

9   THE CAT AND THE CANARY in 1939?

10   THE NUN AND THE SERGEANT in 1962?

11 THE COWBOY AND THE LADY in 1939?

12 THE MODEL AND THE MARRIAGE BROKER in 1952?

13 FREEBIE AND THE BEAN in 1974?

14 THE CISCO KID AND THE LADY in 1940?

15 THE MAJOR AND THE MINOR in 1942?

16 THE PROUD AND THE PROFANE in 1956?

17 THE GYPSY AND THE GENTLEMAN in 1957?

18 PRIDE AND PREJUDICE in 1940?

19 THE PRINCE AND THE PAUPER in 1937?

20 THE DOCTOR AND THE GIRL in 1949?

FLYNN OF BURMA (Easy)

In which film did Errol Flynn:

1 Play a role subsequently played by Doug McClure?

2 Play an Indian?

3 Wear hornrimmed glasses?

4 Dress up as Santa Claus?

5 Take part in a gunfight in the Alamo?

6 Play a French criminal condemned to the guillotine?

7 Capture Nazis in the Canadian arctic?

8 Play a Norwegian patriot?

9 Play a medical researcher into aviation hazards?

10 Expose a murderous dentist?

11 Duel with Henry Daniell (and his double)?

12 Defeat Humphrey Bogart, who was playing a half-breed outlaw?

13 Take a role originally played by Richard Barthelmess?

14 Kill Alan Hale in a duel?

15 Get murdered?

EGO (Medium)

Name the actor or actress playing the 'I' of the following films.

1 I WAS AN AMERICAN SPY

2 I REMEMBER MAMA

3 I WAS A MALE WAR BRIDE

4 I KNOW WHERE I'M GOING

5 I WAS A TEENAGE WEREWOLF

6 I WANT TO LIVE

7 I MET HIM IN PARIS

8 I MARRIED A MONSTER FROM OUTER SPACE

9 I MARRIED A WITCH

10 I AM THE LAW

11 IF I WERE KING

12 I AM A CAMERA

13 I'LL CRY TOMORROW

14 I LOVED A WOMAN

15 I AM SUZANNE

WOMEN! (Easy)

Who played each of the following women?

1 WOMAN CHASES MAN

2 THE WOMAN IN WHITE

3 WOMAN OF THE RIVER

4 WOMAN OF THE YEAR (1942)

5 THE WOMAN ON THE BEACH

6 MARKED WOMAN

7 THE WOMAN IN THE WINDOW

8 WOMAN ON THE RUN

9 WOMAN IN HIDING

10 SINGAPORE WOMAN

11 WHITE WOMAN

12 WOMAN IN A DRESSING GOWN

13 INVISIBLE WOMAN

14 SPIDER WOMAN

15 THE MIRACLE WOMAN

16 RED HEADED WOMAN

17 A WOMAN ALONE

18 THE WOMAN I LOVE

19 THE WOMAN IN QUESTION (FIVE ANGLES ON MURDER)

20 A WOMAN'S FACE

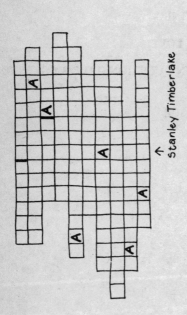

Small town doctor
Irish horse-trainer
Cousin George
Exasperated employer
Defence lawyer
Paranoic composer
Deceived spouse
Lady in waiting
Cigarette lighter
Nagging mother

↑ Stanley Timberlake

Laddergram 9

92

BETTER KNOWN AS (Easy)

Simon Templar is a character better known as THE
SAINT. As what series characters would the following
be more familiar?

1 Mrs Dagwood Bumstead

2 Michael Lanyard

3 Nick Charles

4 Robert Ordway

5 Carmelita Lindsay

6 Lawrence Talbot

7 Simon Sparrow

8 Bruce Wayne

THE FILM AND THE FACE (Medium)

Name the film in which each of the following characters played a leading role, and say what actor played the part.

1   Cody Jarrett

2   Wallace Wooley

3   Adrienne Fromsett

4   Enrique Claudin

5   Holly Martins

6   Walter Neff

7   Yancey Cravat (1930)

8   Sydney Fairfield (1932)

9   Percy Blakeney (1934)

10 Henriette Deluzy-Desportes

11 Tony Camonte

12 Brigid O'Shaughnessy (1940)

13 Enrico Bandello

14 Mortimer Brewster

15 Charles Condomine

16 Elizabeth Bennet

17 Jefferson Smith

18 Geoffrey T. Spaulding

19 Jedediah Leland

20 Marcus Superbus

21 Regina Giddens

22 Tom Joad

23 Arthur Seaton

24 Violet Venable

25 Harold Bissonette

NOT SO FUNNY (Easy)

Here are some of the less successful films of well-known comedians. Which comedians?

1 WELCOME DANGER

2 DANCE WITH ME HENRY

3 THE ROGUE SONG

4 JUST MY LUCK

5 A DOG'S LIFE

6 BATTLING BUTLER

7 MAN ABOUT TOWN

8 ON THE DOUBLE

9 DANDY DICK

10 THE OLD FASHIONED WAY

11 WE'RE GOING TO BE RICH

12 OH SAILOR BEHAVE

13 HOOTS, MON

14 THE FARMER'S DAUGHTER (1940)

15 SOME LIKE IT HOT (1939)

16 FORTY LITTLE MOTHERS

17 THE BIG MOUTH

18 GET CRACKING

19 EARTHWORM TRACTORS

20 STRAIGHT, PLACE AND SHOW

Poster 9. Name the missing film title.

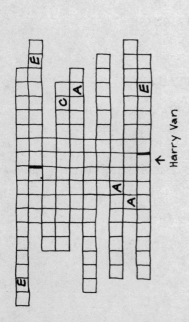

Singer
Seaman
Teacher
Oil man
Judge Cotton
Procrastinator
Anthropologist's wife
Susan
Divorcee
Fellow hitchhiker

Harry Van

Laddergram 10

THE MURDERER IS IN THIS ROOM (Medium)

Who played the murderer in the following whodunits?

1 GREEN FOR DANGER

2 AFTER THE THIN MAN

3 THE MALTESE FALCON (of Miles Archer) (1940)

4 LAURA

5 THE SPIRAL STAIRCASE

6 CROSSFIRE

7 THE LADY IN THE LAKE

8 THE LIST OF ADRIAN MESSENGER

9 THE SCARLET CLAW

10 THE HOUND OF THE BASKERVILLES (Rathbone 1939 version)

11 HARPER

12 AND THEN THERE WERE NONE (1945)

13 THE GHOST BREAKERS

14 TOPPER RETURNS

15 THE CAT AND THE CANARY (1939)

16 CHARLIE CHAN AT TREASURE ISLAND

17 THE KENNEL MURDER CASE

18 HOT SPOT / I WAKE UP SCREAMING

19 THE GREENE MURDER CASE (1929)

20 THE NAKED CITY

21 WITNESS FOR THE PROSECUTION

22 DIAL M FOR MURDER

23 THE LODGER (1944)

24 STAGE FRIGHT

25 FRENZY

FREDERIC IS COMPOSING TONIGHT (Easy)

Name the film, and the composer played by each actor, in the year given.

1   Robert Alda in 1945

2   Cary Grant in 1945

3   Robert Walker in 1947

4   Jean-Pierre Aumont in 1947

5   Dirk Bogarde in 1960

6   Alan Badel in 1956

7   Paul Henried in 1947

8   Richard Tauber in 1934

9   Wilfred Lawson in 1942

10 Maurice Evans in 1953

11 Nat King Cole in 1957

12 Jose Ferrer in 1954

13 Richard Chamberlain in 1970

14 Jean-Louis Barrault in 1940

15 Fernand Gravet in 1938

16 Walter Connolly in 1939

17 Robert Walker in 1946

18 Don Ameche in 1939

19 Toralv Maurstad in 1970

20 Gordon Macrae, Ernest Borgnine and Dan Dailey in 1956

21 Fred Astaire and Red Skelton in 1952

22 Victor Mature in 1942

23 Tom Drake and Mickey Rooney in 1948

24 Clifton Webb in 1952

25 Carl Boehm in 1960

OH, JOHNNY, OH (Easy)

In the following films, who played Johnny?

1 JOHNNY COOL

2 JOHNNY GUITAR

3 JOHNNY O'CLOCK

4 JOHNNY CONCHO

5 JOHNNY DARK

6 JOHNNY COME LATELY

7 JOHNNY ALLEGRO

8 JOHNNY EAGER

9 JOHNNY TREMAIN

10 NO LOVE FOR JOHNNIE

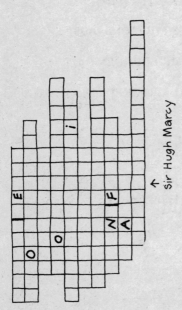

Brother
Native
Diver
Politician
Gypsy
Intended victim
Villain
Nurse
Lover
Journalist

← Sir Hugh Marcy

105

MORE THAN ONE TALENT (Medium)

The following films were directed by people at least equally well-known as actors. Can you name them?

1   THE GANGSTER STORY (1958)

2   THE CONQUEROR (1956)

3   NIGHT OF THE HUNTER (1955)

4   MISS TATLOCK'S MILLIONS (1948)

5   THE AMAZING MR BLUNDEN (1972)

6   SKY WEST AND CROOKED (1966) (U.S title: GYPSY GIRL)

7   MADAME X (1929)

8   TIME LIMIT (1957)

9   SHORT CUT TO HELL (1957)

10 TAM LIN (1970)

11 BREEZY (1973)

12 DIE VERLORENE (1950)

13 CHARLIE BUBBLES (1967)

14 A MAN ALONE (1955)

15 A GUIDE FOR THE MARRIED MAN (1967)

16 THE LADY IN THE LAKE (1947)

17 RUNNING SCARED (1972)

18 ANTONY AND CLEOPATRA (1971)

19 ON APPROVAL (1944)

20 KOTCH (1971)

21 BUCK AND THE PREACHER (1971)

22 MY TRUE STORY (1951)

23 YOUNG WINSTON (1972)

24 THE LOST MOMENT (1948)

25 THE SECRET FURY (1950)

26 THE GREAT MAN (1956)

27 LITTLE MURDERS (1971)

28 RACHEL, RACHEL (1968)

29 DEAD RINGER (1964)

30 THE KENTUCKIAN (1955)

31 NONE BUT THE BRAVE (1965)

32 MAN TRAP (1961)

33 HOME AT SEVEN (1953) (US title: MURDER ON MONDAY)

34 BEACH RED (1967)

35 THE CEREMONY (1963)

UNIVERSAL PRESENTS

A TITANIC TROPICAL FROLIC..
race-paced with laughs and lu-WOW lovelies

BUD **ABBOTT**
and LOU
COSTELLO

with
VIRGINIA BRUCE
ROBERT PAIGE
LEIF ERIKSON
Marie (THE BODY) McDONALD
Lionel Atwill Nan Wynn
THE FOUR INK SPOTS

Poster 10. Name the missing film title.

THEY SUFFERED A SEA CHANGE (II) (Medium)

Here are titles of British films as they were released in America. Name the original British titles.

1 IMMORTAL BATTALION (1944)

2 THE RAPE OF MALAYA (1956)

3 THE CREEPING UNKNOWN (1955)

4 THE GOLDEN VIRGIN (1957)

5 STAIRWAY TO HEAVEN (1945)

6 AFRICAN FURY (1952)

7 HAUNTED HONEYMOON (1940)

8 THE PROMOTER (1952)

9 DIE DIE MY DARLING (1965)

10 SPITFIRE (1942)

11 MISTER V (1941)

12 JOHNNY IN THE CLOUDS (1945)

13 THE CONQUEROR WORM (1968)

14 THE GIRL WAS YOUNG (1938)

15 A WOMAN ALONE (1937)

16 TIGHT LITTLE ISLAND (1949)

17 DESERT ATTACK (1958)

18 MAN OF EVIL (1944)

19 THE DETECTIVE (1954)

20 PURSUIT OF THE GRAF SPEE (1956)

DEAR MR GABLE (Easy)

In what film did Clark Gable:

1   Romance Carole Lombard?

2   Play a boxer in love with a musical comedy star?

3   Escape from a New Guinea penal colony?

4   Befriend an Indian chief played by Jack Holt?

5   Fall for a girl named Snapshot?

6   Help a friend search for his soul and pray for a baby's life?

7   Contend with William Boyd for the hand of Helen Twelvetrees?

8   Catch a night bus from Miami towards New York?

9   Captain a ship heading for Hong Kong?

10 Play Blackie Norton?

11 Perform a song-and-dance act with a troupe of six girls?

12 Play an Irish patriot?

13 Smuggle a girl out of Russia? (Two possible answers)

14 Play a newsreel photographer?

15 Play an advertising executive?

16 Play a mayor?

17 Defend Texas against the Mexicans?

18 Play a role previously taken by Herbert Marshall and
    Bing Crosby?

19 Play a jewel thief?

20 Die in the arms of Helen Hayes?

THE TOPIC IS BIOPICS (Medium)

In each of the following cases, say what actor or entertainer was impersonated in what film by the person given.

1   Jill Clayburgh in 1976

2   Betty Hutton in 1945

3   Charles Ruggles in 1944

4   Brian Aherne in 1937

5   Carroll Baker in 1964

6   Miriam Hopkins in 1941

7   Keefe Brasselle in 1953

8   Richard Burton in 1954

9   Susan Hayward in 1955

10 Donald O'Connor in 1957

11 Errol Flynn in 1958

12 Danny Kaye in 1959

13 Rod Steiger in 1976

14 Kim Novak in 1957

15 James Cagney in 1957

16 Betty Hutton in 1947

17 Tony Curtis in 1953

18 Alice Faye in 1940

19 Doris Day in 1955

20 June Haver in 1949

21 June Haver and Betty Grable in 1944

22 Tommy Trinder in 1944

23 Sal Mineo in 1960

24 Ann Blyth in 1954

25 Patrice Munsel in 1950

26 Ann Sheridan in 1944

27 Betty Hutton in 1953

28 Natalie Wood in 1962

29 Diana Ross in 1974

30 Frank Sinatra in 1957

N.B. The term entertainer is used in its broadest sense

SILENCE PLEASE II (Difficult)

1   Who played the title role in Lubitsch's 1919 German film of MADAME DU BARRY? (She later rose to Hollywood fame.)

2   British film-maker George Pearson starred Betty Balfour in a series of twenties comedies about a cockney girl called . . . ?

3   Greta Garbo in 1925 appeared in a German film directed by G. W. Pabst. Name it.

4   Eisenstein's Odessa Steps sequence is a famous piece of film editing. From what 1925 film does it come?

5   In 1927 Walter Ruttmann made a film subtitled "the symphony of a great city". The title of the film was the name of the city. Which city?

6   In 1926 Alfred Hitchcock directed Ivor Novello in a film based vaguely on the Jack the Ripper murders, updated from a novel by Mrs Belloc-Lowndes. Title, please.

7   In 1927 Anthony Asquith and A. V. Bramble co-directed a drama set behind the scenes at a film studio. What was it called?

8   In 1928 Luis Bunuel and Salvador Dali made a surrealist film which began with a girl's eye apparently being cut by a razor. Name the film.

9   In 1919 Mauritz Stiller directed a famous story by Selma Lagerlof about three plundering mercenaries of the sixteenth century. Title, please.

10   In 1920 Benjamin Christensen of Sweden made a vivid account of pagan rituals, mixing fiction with instructional documentary. The original title is HAXAN; by what English title is the film usually known?

11 In 1924 in Germany, F. W. Murnau directed DER LETZTE MANN or THE LAST LAUGH, about a hotel doorman demoted to lavatory attendant. Who played the leading role?

12 In the following year the same actor appeared with Lya de Putti in a "backstage" drama known by one title in Great Britain and another in America. Give both.

13 Name the 1926 film by Henrik Galeen in which Conrad Veidt played a man haunted by his own mirror-image.

14 In 1926 Brigitte Helm played a robot girl in a futuristic fantasy directed by Fritz Lang. Title, please.

15 Miss Helm also played a blind girl in a 1927 film by G. W. Pabst. What was it?

16 Name the actress who played the title role in Carl Dreyer's 1928 film THE PASSION OF JOAN OF ARC.

17 Twenty five years in anticipation of Cinerama, Abel Gance in 1927 used a triple screen. For what film?

18 Who wrote THE CABINET OF DR CALIGARI (1919)? (2 marks)

19 In France in 1928 Germaine Dulac made a Freudian film about the sexual repressions of a young priest. Name it.

20 PARIS QUI DORT (1923) and ENTR'ACTE (1924) are among the early comedies of which celebrated French director?

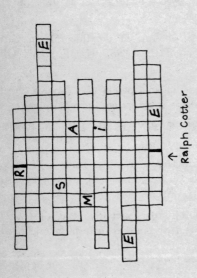

king
Soldier
FBI
Stranded entertainer
Ruth
Moll
Tycoon's daughter
Alcoholic
Lieutenant
Vaudevillian
Dancer

Ralph Cotter

Laddergram 12.

118

Old actor
Male impersonator
con woman
Famous 'doctor'
Murderer
Daisy
Doctor
Inventor
Western wife
Ex-president

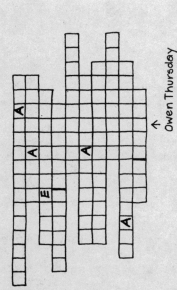

↑
Owen Thursday

Laddergram 13

COLOURS OF THE RAINBOW (Easy)

Films often have colourful titles. For the following fifteen films, supply the colour.

1 THE FUZZY ...... NIGHTGOWN

2 THE ...... DANUBE (1949)

3 THE MAN IN THE ...... SUIT

4 ...... PLANET MARS

5 THE ...... GARDENIA

6 ...... SKY

7 THE ...... MASK

8 THE ...... JUNGLE

9 ...... TUESDAY

10 ...... BANNERS

11 THE ...... HOUSE

12 ...... FIRE

13 THE ...... KIMONO

14 ...... ANGEL (1952)

15 BIG ......

Now for fifteen in which the colour is given; but supply the missing word.

16 ...... SCARLET

17 THE ...... WORE BLACK

18 THE ...... WORE RED

19 ...... IN A GOLDEN EYE

20 ...... WITH RED HAIR

21 THE ...... IN GREEN

22 THE ...... IN GREY

23 NAVY BLUE AND ......

24 THE ...... IN WHITE

25 RED ...... AND BLUE

26 ...... AMBER

27 BLUE, WHITE AND ......

28 BLACK MARKET ......

29 ...... OVER THE WHITE HOUSE

30 BLUE ......, WHITE ......

DEBUTANTES (Difficult)

What stars made their first feature film appearances in the following movies?

1 RED HAIRED ALIBI (1932)

2 THE PAINTED DESERT (1931)

3 GRAND OLD GIRL (1935)

4 FIGHTER SQUADRON (1948)

5 LATE EXTRA (1935)

6 TALL STORY (1960)

7 UP THE RIVER (1930)

8 TAMMY AND THE DOCTOR (1963)

9 GOLDEN BOY (1939)

10 LAS VEGAS NIGHTS (1941)

11 THE STRANGE LOVE OF MARTHA IVERS (1946)

12 CLAUDIA (1943)

13 THE MALTESE FALCON (1941)

14 NIGHT AFTER NIGHT (1932)

15 HEAVEN WITH A BARBED WIRE FENCE (1939)

16 THE TROUBLE WITH HARRY (1955)

17 FOUR DAUGHTERS (1938)

18 PORT OF NEW YORK (1949)

19 FOR ME AND MY GAL (1942)

20 DARK CITY (1950)

21 THE INVISIBLE MAN (1933)

22 NO WAY OUT (1950)

23 A DEVIL WITH WOMEN (1930)

24 THE KILLERS (1945)

25 ESTHER WATERS (1947)

26 THIS IS THE NIGHT (1932)

27 THE SPECKLED BAND (1931)

28 THE QUEEN OF SPADES (1948)

29 LASSIE COME HOME (1943)

30 BAD SISTER (1931)

UNLIKELY BEHAVIOUR (Medium)

In what film did:

1   Ralph Richardson play a villainous vicar?

2   Nigel Bruce appear as a strong man?

3   Basil Rathbone sing a music hall song?

4   James Mason play a Chinese?

5   James Stewart turn out to be the murderer?

6   Rex Harrison pretend to be a Gestapo officer?

7   Leslie Howard pretend to be an old lady?

8   Lionel Barrymore pretend to be an old lady?

9   George Sanders disguise himself as a woman?

10 Lon Chaney Jnr as the wolf man get himself cured and romantically attached?

11 John Barrymore become a circus acrobat?

12 Gale Sondergaard turn into a cat?

13 Mickey Rooney play a Japanese?

14 Edmund Gwenn play a professional murderer?

15 Humphrey Bogart play a vampire?

16 Marlene Dietrich make her entrance in a gorilla skin?

17 Anne Bancroft play a murderer?

18 Roland Young play a strangler?

19 Alice Faye get a pie in the face?

20 Reginald Denny turn into a monster?

21 Agnes Moorehead play a centenarian?

22 Mischa Auer impersonate a gorilla?

23 Fredric March sock Carole Lombard on the jaw?

24 Adolphe Menjou take part in a battle of fireworks?

25 Katharine Hepburn fall into a canal?

26 Joel McCrea join the chain gang?

27 Betty Hutton have sextuplets?

28 Dame May Whitty play a spy?

29 Groucho Marx play a historical personage?

30 Buster Keaton drive a bus?

Poster 11. Name the missing film title.

HUMBLE BEGINNINGS (Easy)

What stars made their names in the following roles, and in what films?

1 An oriental potentate with many children.

2 A national celebrity who wreaks havoc in the home of Mr and Mrs Stanley.

3 A dramatic critic fired for writing an honest review.

4 A waspish columnist who typed in his bath.

5 A Mr Caspar Gutman, one of several people in pursuit of a *rara avis*.

6 A psychopathic murderer known only by an initial.

7 A scientist named Griffin whose discovery, self administered, gave him megalomania.

8 A frustrated bicycle factory worker who enjoyed his weekends.

9 An Irishman working as a Nazi spy in London during World War Two.

10 A night club singer who married a teacher named Immanuel Rath.

11 A radio detective named The Fox.

12 A hired assassin named Raven.

OLD NICK (Easy)

Who played the Devil – or his emissary – in the following?

1 THE DEVIL WITH HITLER
2 LES VISITEURS DU SOIR
3 CABIN IN THE SKY
4 HEAVEN CAN WAIT
5 ANGEL ON MY SHOULDER
6 THE STORY OF MANKIND
7 DAMN YANKEES
8 TALES FROM THE CRYPT
9 ALL THAT MONEY CAN BUY
10 MEET MR LUCIFER
11 THE SORROWS OF SATAN
12 ALIAS NICK BEAL

FATEFUL MEETINGS (Medium)

Who met who, in what film:

1 On a night train from San Francisco to Los Angeles, when he stole from her purse?

2 In an old mansion when she mistook him for an undertaker?

3 In a blazing hotel when she had no clothes on?

4 On his first trip to Europe, at night on the top deck of the Queen Mary?

5 While crossing a street in Paris, on her first night in town?

6 On a street at night, when he got splashed with mud on his way to a furniture warehouse?

7 In a western saloon when he poured water on her?

8 On a Chicago-bound train when he was hunted by police?

9 In her parlour on the afternoon before her wedding, her ex-husband having introduced him as a friend of her absent brother?

10 At a ball when she had heard him say that there was not a young woman in the room he would gladly stand up with?

11 In a Monte Carlo hotel when her older companion had forced an introduction?

12 In a Hollywood diner when he is trying to lose his identity and she has given up being an actress?

YOU DIRTY RAT (Easy)

In which film did James Cagney:

1 Constantly hitch his shoulders?

2 Join the Canadian Air Corps?

3 Bring in a banana crop?

4 Stage live prologues for movie theatres?

5 Promote a grapefruit diet?

6 Philosophise in a bar?

7 Become president of a longshoremen's union?

8 Train O.S.S. undercover agents?

9 Get himself jailed for vagrancy?

10 Extract his co-star from a cactus patch?

11 Play a dentist?

12 Become a coward in the front line during World War One?

13 Play a Hollywood scriptwriter?

14 Co-star with Edward G. Robinson?

15 Play a movie theatre usher?

Poster 12. Name the missing film title.

WHO NEEDS *TWO* STARS? (Medium)

In the case of each of these well-known films, give the star (easy) and the co-star of the opposite sex (difficult).

1 APACHE

2 THE NAKED MAJA

3 DON JUAN (1926)

4 THE SINGING FOOL

5 THE SCARLET EMPRESS

6 BEN HUR (1926)

7 BEN HUR (1959)

8 THE SCARLET LETTER (1927)

9 STELLA DALLAS (1937)

10 ACROSS THE WIDE MISSOURI

11 THE SEA HAWK (1940)

12 IT

13 THE LITTLE MINISTER

14 BIG JIM McLAIN

15 THE SEVENTH CROSS

16 THE BIG SHOT

17 WHERE LOVE HAS GONE

18 MATA HARI (1931)

19 RAFFLES (1940)

20 THE PRIDE OF THE YANKEES

21 MY LIFE WITH CAROLINE

22 KNOCK ON WOOD

23 LOST HORIZON (1937)

24 YANKEE DOODLE DANDY

25 FOREIGN CORRESPONDENT

TRIPLE TROUBLE I (Easy)

Name the films described. Each one has the word THREE in the title.

1 The problems of an irresponsible Brooklyn family.

2 A lady journalist asks her daughters' permission to marry again.

3 Girls in Rome fall in love.

4 Three sisters go to California to find millionaire husbands.

5 After World War Two, a Jap-hating sergeant falls in love with a Japanese girl.

6 A sweepstake ticket produces fortune and ill-fortune for its investors.

7 Agnes Newton Keith tries to escape from Borneo during World War Two.

8 A naval civil servant is dismissed as a security risk.

9 Daughters break up their father's planned remarriage.

10 Dr Gillespie has new interns.

11 The song-writing career of Bert Kalmar and Harry Ruby.

12 A salesman has a brief affair with a girl who later moves into his home.

13 A greeting card writer picks racetrack winners.

14 A lawman gets an outlaw on the right train despite the menacing presence of his gang.

Fugitive
Missionary
Wife
Servant
Slave
Gypsy
Daughter
Dancer
Wife
Employer
Naval officer
Host
Bather
Dancer
Bootmaker

↑ J J Bealler

Laddergram 14

135

THE FAMILY HOUR (Difficult)

Who played:

1 Ryan O'Neal's father in LOVE STORY?

2 Bette Davis' mother in NOW VOYAGER?

3 Vivien Leigh's father in GONE WITH THE WIND?

4 Janet Gaynor's grandmother in A STAR IS BORN?

5 Freddie Bartholemew's aunt in DAVID COPPER-FIELD?

6 Juanita Moore's daughter in IMITATION OF LIFE?

7 Elizabeth Taylor's husband in ASH WEDNESDAY?

8 Rosalind Russell's sister in MY SISTER EILEEN?

9 Eugene Pallette's wife in HEAVEN CAN WAIT?

10 Greer Garson's husband in MADAME CURIE?

11 Dana Andrews' wife in THE BEST YEARS OF OUR LIVES?

12 Anne Bancroft's husband in THE GRADUATE?

13 Deanna Durbin's father in ONE HUNDRED MEN AND A GIRL?

14 Katharine Hepburn's father in THE PHILADELPHIA STORY?

15 Greer Garson's mother in PRIDE AND PREJUDICE?

16 Joan Crawford's daughter in MILDRED PIERCE?

17 Richard Haydn's mother in CLUNY BROWN?

18 Paul Muni's sister in SCARFACE?

19 Robert Taylor's wife in CONSPIRATOR?

20 Walter Huston's wife in DODSWORTH?

21 Gladys Cooper's husband in REBECCA?

22 Lionel Barrymore's grandson in ON BORROWED TIME?

23 Paul Muni's wife in THE GOOD EARTH?

24 Bette Davis' husband in JUAREZ?

25 Ronald Colman's brother in LOST HORIZON?

26 Katharine Hepburn's sister in HOLIDAY?

27 Raymond Massey's wife in THE OLD DARK HOUSE?

28 Betty Hutton's sister in THE MIRACLE OF MORGANS CREEK?

29 Celia Johnson's husband in BRIEF ENCOUNTER?

30 Orson Welles' father in CITIZEN KANE?

31 James Stewart's sister in HARVEY?

32 Ernest Thesiger's sister, brother and father in THE OLD DARK HOUSE?

33 Al Jolson's father in THE JAZZ SINGER?

34 Oliver Hardy's wife in SONS OF THE DESERT?

35 Laurence Olivier's wife in WUTHERING HEIGHTS?

36 Edward Everett Horton's wife in TOP HAT?

37 Genevieve Tobin's husband in ONE HOUR WITH YOU?

38 James Cagney's father in THE STRAWBERRY BLONDE?

39 Claude Rains' daughter in KINGS ROW?

40 Susan Hayward's father in I MARRIED A WITCH?

41 Henry Fonda's mother in THE GRAPES OF WRATH?

42 Albert Finney's wife in CHARLIE BUBBLES?

43 Errol Flynn's father in THAT FORSYTE WOMAN?

44 Rosalind Russell's brother in MOURNING BECOMES ELECTRA?

45 Jean Arthur's mother in YOU CAN'T TAKE IT WITH YOU?

46 Mickey Rooney's aunt in A FAMILY AFFAIR?

47 Agnes Moorehead's nephew in THE MAGNIFICENT AMBERSONS?

48 Colin Clive's father in FRANKENSTEIN?

49 Carole Lombard's mother in MY MAN GODFREY?

50 Dean Stockwell's grandfather in THE GREEN YEARS?

51 Joseph Cotten's niece in SHADOW OF A DOUBT?

52 David Niven's wife in MURDER BY DEATH?

Poster 13. Name the missing film title.

MORE STARS THAN THERE ARE IN THE SKY
(Easy)

All-star extravaganzas, in which the studio used to co-opt all the stars on the payroll for walk-ons, were seldom artistic successes, but they usually provided their share of memorable moments. Can you name the film in which:

1 John Barrymore recited RICHARD III?

2 Bing Crosby sang OLD GLORY?

3 Eddie Cantor sang HAVING A PATRIOTIC TIME?

4 Fanny Brice appeared in her sketch THE SWEEP-STAKE TICKET?

5 Maurice Chevalier sang ALL I WANT IS A GIRL LIKE YOU in a park in Paris?

6 Bing Crosby made his debut, as one of the Rhythm Boys?

7 Paulette Goddard, Dorothy Lamour and Veronica Lake sang A SWEATER, A SARONG AND A PEEK-A-BOO BANG?

8 Jack Benny performed a routine with Laurel and Hardy?

9 Orson Welles sawed Marlene Dietrich in half?

10 Bette Davis sang THEY'RE EITHER TOO YOUNG OR TOO OLD?

FROM THE ORIGINAL NOVEL (Easy)

Name the films made from these novels.

1 BENIGHTED by J. B. Priestley

2 THE BRICK FOXHOLE by Richard Brooks

3 THE OFF-ISLANDERS by Nathaniel Benchley

4 THE WHEEL SPINS by Ethel Lina White

5 SOME MUST WATCH by Ethel Lina White

6 YOUR ARKANSAS TRAVELLER by Budd Schulberg

7 ROGUE MALE by Geoffrey Household

8 THE CURSE OF CAPISTRANO by Johnstone McCulley

9 THE HOUSE OF DR EDWARDES by Francis Beeding

10 THE CLANSMAN by Thomas Dixon

11 FROM AMONG THE DEAD by Boileau and Narcejac

12 HOLD AUTUMN IN YOUR HAND by George Sessions Perry

13   THE PHANTOM CROWN by Bertita Harding

14   A SHILLING FOR CANDLES by Josephine Tey

15   MUTE WITNESS by Robert L. Pike

16   RED ALERT by Peter George

17   BEFORE THE FACT by Francis Iles

18   THE NUTMEG TREE by Margery Sharp

19   MAMA'S BANK ACCOUNT by Kathryn Forbes

20   THE ONCE AND FUTURE KING by T. H. White

21   GLORY FOR ME by Mackinlay Kantor

22   THE LIGHT OF DAY by Eric Ambler

23   MIAMI MAYHEM by Marvin H. Albert

24   A GUN FOR SALE by Graham Greene

25   MAN RUNNING by Selwyn Jepson

WORLD GAZETTEER (Easy)

Name the countries, states or cities omitted from the following film titles.

1 A HIGH WIND IN ......

2 ACTION IN ......

3 THEY CAME TO BLOW UP ......

4 CANDLELIGHT IN ......

5 THE ...... GESTURE

6 JOAN OF ......

7 ...... CANTEEN

8 TONIGHT WE RAID ......

9 MASQUERADE IN ......

10 HOTEL ......

11 MISSION TO ......

12 TEN GENTLEMEN FROM ......

13 THE TUTTLES OF ......

14 THE ...... STRANGLER

15 MISS V FROM ......

16 NIGHT TRAIN TO ......

17 THE LAST TRAIN FROM ......

18 LITTLE OLD ......

19 I MET HIM IN ......

20 DOUGHBOYS IN ......

21 FOG OVER ......

22 BACK TO ......

23 ...... I LOVE YOU

24 HELLO ...... HELLO

25 TWO YANKS IN ......

N.B. All these films were made before 1950.

ANATOMY (Easy)

Complete the following film titles by adding in each
case one word describing a portion of human or animal
anatomy.

1 BELLES ON THEIR ......

2 CAREFUL SOFT ......

3 BIG BROWN ......

4 THE SCREAMING ......

5 THE HIDDEN ......

6 DONOVAN'S ......

7 ...... AT THE WINDOW

8 DREAMING ......

9 TOM ......

10 THE ...... BEACH STORY

11 THE ...... OF MARBLE

12 DEAD MAN'S ......

13 CLAIRE'S ......

14 MILLION DOLLAR ......

15 THE SCARLET ......

16 ...... TO BATAAN

17 THE ...... OF FU MANCHU

18 ...... IN THE NIGHT

19 ...... OF THE RIPPER

20 ...... OF THE DEVIL

21 ...... OF A FUGITIVE

22 ...... IN ...... (same word repeated)

23 CAPTAIN LIGHT......

24 ...... OF THE CAT

25 THE MUMMY'S ......

BIOPICS AGAIN (Easy)

The following people, all real, had films based on their lives. Name in each case the profession or calling of the person, the film, and the actor who played him or her.

1   Douglas Bader

2   Gus Kahn

3   Violette Szabo

4   Red Nichols

5   George M. Cohan

6   Alfred the Great

7   Hiram Maxim

8   Paul Ehrlich

9   Grover Cleveland Alexander

10 Alexander Graham Bell

11 Amy Johnson

12 Jenny Lind

13 Jane Froman

14 William Friese-Greene

15 Peg Woffington

16 Marjorie Laurence

17 Vesta Tilley

18 John Montgomery

19 Guy Gabaldon

20 Ernie Pyle

21 Robert Stroud

22 Sol Hurok

23 Barbara Graham

24 John Paul Jones

25 Eva Tanguay

26 Eddie Foy

27 R. J. Mitchell

28 Grace Moore

29 Thomas More

30 Gladys Aylward

ACTORS IN COMMON (Difficult)

What do the following actors have in common, as far as film roles are concerned? Two marks for each question.

1 Edward Everett Horton, Bob Hope, Charles Laughton

2 Sheldon Lewis, Paul Massie, Spencer Tracy

3 Fredric March, Cedric Hardwicke, Maria Casares

4 Ilona Massey, Cedric Hardwicke, Basil Rathbone

5 Melvyn Douglas, Lew Ayres, Charles Boyer, John Gilbert, Fredric March

6 Henry Fonda, Raymond Massey, Walter Huston

7 George Montgomery, Elliott Gould, Robert Montgomery

8 Paulette Goddard, Claire Bloom, Martha Raye, Dawn Addams

9 Bette Davis, Tallulah Bankhead, Elizabeth Bergner

10 Charles Boyer, Ray Milland, Joseph Cotten, Ralph Richardson, Trevor Howard

11 Joan Fontaine, Jack Lemmon, Susan Hayward, Ray Milland

12 Bette Davis, Ronald Colman, Olivia de Havilland, Douglas Fairbanks Jnr

13 Charles Laughton, Anthony Quinn, Lon Chaney

14 Donald Cook, Eddie Quillan, Ralph Bellamy, William Gargan

15 Red Skelton, Stuart Erwin, Creighton Hale

16 Lyn Harding, George Zucco, Henry Daniell

17 Barry K. Barnes, David Niven, Leslie Howard

18 Joan Fontaine, Rosamund John, Jean Arless, Diane Baker

19 Charles Boyer, Herbert Lom, Rod Steiger

20 Herbert Lom, Lon Chaney, Claude Rains

21 Irene Dunne, Samantha Eggar, Deborah Kerr

22 Cedric Hardwicke, Peter Finch, Laurence Olivier

23 Anthony Quinn, Alec Guinness, Rex Harrison

24 Claude Rains, Louis Calhern, Warren William

25 Nick Adams, Lawrence Tierney, Warren Oates

26 Danny Kaye, Michael Redgrave, Erich von Stroheim

27 Louis Hayward, George Sanders, Jean Marais

28 Bernard Punsley, Bobby Jordan, Gabriel Dell

29 Ronald Colman, John Howard, Richard Johnson

30 Glenn Strange, Kiwi Kingston, Bela Lugosi

NUMBERS (Medium)

A number is missing from the title of each of the following films, all made before 1950. Supply it.

1 ...... STRANGERS

2 ...... CAME BACK

3 ...... MEN AND A GIRL

4 OVER ......

5 ...... MEN AND A PRAYER

6 ...... GIRLS AND A SAILOR

7 PILOT NUMBER ......

8 ...... SINNERS

9 ...... GRAVES TO CAIRO

10 ...... NIGHTS

11 ...... SECONDS

12 THE SECRET ......

13 ...... SISTERS FROM BOSTON

14 ...... MEN IN WHITE

15 ...... LITTLE GIRLS IN BLUE

16 ...... SMART PEOPLE

17 ...... HEARTS FOR JULIA

18 ...... HORSEMEN

19 ...... WIVES

20 ...... MOTHERS

21 ...... FATHERS

22 ...... GODFATHERS

23 ...... SONS

24 ...... DAUGHTERS

25 ...... GIRLS

26 ...... YEARS IN SING SING

27 ...... SECONDS OVER TOKYO

28 THE ...... STEPS

29 RENDEZVOUS ......

30 ABROAD WITH ...... YANKS

SUCH COMMON WORDS (Easy)

Supply the one word which is missing from the following groups of titles. All the films are first features: no age limit.

1 PARIS ......: FAMILY ......: ...... FOR THREE

2 IT'S ...... I'M AFTER: APPOINTMENT FOR ......: ...... CRAZY

3 THEY CAME TO A ......: ...... FOR CONQUEST: ...... STREETS

4 ESCAPE IN THE ......: ...... FURY: THE PAINTED ......

5 HIRED ......; FIRED ......: BEHOLD MY ......

6 ...... GIRL: THE ......; THE WILD ......

7 MR ......: ...... FOR MILLIONS: THE ...... LOVERS

8 THE ...... CHANGES: ......'S END: UP THE ......

9 ...... OF EVENTS: THE ...... : NIGHT ......

10 ...... ON TRIAL: OUR ......: ...... WITHOUT PITY

11 A STOLEN ......: A DOUBLE ......: ...... RETURNS

12 THE ...... PEOPLE: ...... COMMAND: ...... PATROL

13 NO TIME FOR ......: THE ...... MAN: THE HUMAN ......

14 ...... OF STRANGERS: ...... OF BAMBOO: ......
OF NUMBERS

15 ...... THE SUN: ...... THAT DREAM: ...... THE
BOYS

16 THE ......'S OUR HOME: NEW ......: OVER
THE ......

17 THE ...... DAWN: ...... ALIBI: ...... CITY

18 THRILL OF A ......: ...... ON THE HIGH SEAS:
AN AMERICAN ......

19 ...... HAPPY: PARTY ......: THE ......
HUNTERS

20 ...... OF SURRENDER: ...... WITHOUT END:
THE DESERT ......

21 LOVE ......: THE DEADLY ......: TOP SECRET
......

22 THE ...... BELOW: BELOVED ......: PUBLIC
......

23 THE ...... YEARS: ...... FIRE: THE ......GLOVE

24 STAR SPANGLED ......: BROADWAY ......: ......
ON THE RIVER

25 PICK A ......: ...... OF MIDNIGHT: MAKE ME
A ......

FROM THE ORIGINAL STORY (Medium)

Name the films made from these short stories and magazine articles.

1 CHRIST IN CONCRETE by Pietro di Donato

2 THE WISDOM OF EVE by Mary Orr

3 STAGE TO LORDSBURG by Ernest Haycox

4 MADAME LA GIMP by Damon Runton

5 CASTING THE RUNES by M. R. James

6 SPURS by Tod Robbins

7 A CAN OF BEANS by Charles Brackett and Billy Wilder

8 LEININGEN VERSUS THE ANTS by Carl Stephenson

9 THE SHORT HAPPY LIFE OF FRANCIS MACOMBER by Ernest Hemingway

10 THE BASEMENT ROOM by Graham Greene

11 NIGHT BUS by Samuel Hopkins Adams

12 OPERA HAT by Clarence Buddington Kelland

13 THE KILLER by George Scullin

14 PATROL by Philip Macdonald

15 THE KILLING FROST by Max Catto

16 THE SIX NAPOLEONS by Sir Arthur Conan Doyle

17 THE ISLAND OF DR MOREAU by H. G. Wells (1932)

18 THE FOGHORN by Ray Bradbury

19 WHO GOES THERE? by John W. Campbell Jnr

20 THE MUSGRAVE RITUAL by Sir Arthur Conan Doyle

21 THE MAN ON THE LEDGE by Joel Sayre

22 PHILOMEL COTTAGE by Agatha Christie

Poster 14. Name the missing film title.

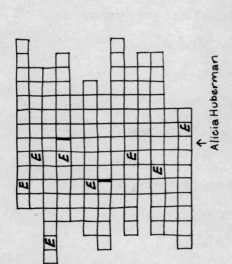

↑ Alicia Huberman

Laddergram 15

Musician
Dowager
Paranoiac
Adam
Neighbour
Oriental
Servant
Pianist
Doctor
Priest
Dentist
Businessman
Mentor

159

COMEBACKS (Medium)

Each of the following films featured the reappearance of a former star who had not been seen on the big screen for at least five years. Name the stars concerned.

1   THE PRIME OF MISS JEAN BRODIE (1969)

2   HI DIDDLE DIDDLE (1943)

3   BERNARDINE (1957)

4   NONE BUT THE LONELY HEART (1944)

5   THE GREAT MAN (1956)

6   STATE FAIR (1962)

7   MADAME X (1966)

8   SOME LIKE IT HOT (1959)

9   WE WERE STRANGERS (1948)

10   SUNSET BOULEVARD (1950)

11   MAD WEDNESDAY (1947)

12   MISTER ROBERTS (1955)

13   HUD (1963)

14 THE NUN AND THE SERGEANT (1962)

15 CRY OF THE BANSHEE (1970)

16 PARRISH (1961)

17 SUMMER WISHES, WINTER DREAMS (1973)

18 SLAVES (1969)

19 THE LAST ANGRY MAN (1959)

20 THE TIME OF INDIFFERENCE (1966)

21 A FEVER IN THE BLOOD (1960)

22 THE APRIL FOOLS (1969)

23 TOM THUMB (1958)

24 RHAPSODY IN BLUE (1945)

25 THE SINGING NUN (1966)

HEROINES AND HEROES (Medium)

In what well-known films were the leading romantic characters named as follows? And who played them?

1 Lady Edwina Esketh and Major Rama Safti

2 Snapshot and Ulysses

3 Henriette Deluzy-Desportes and the Duc de Praslin

4 Laura Jesson and Dr Alec Harvey

5 Judith Traherne and Dr Frederick Steele

6 Maggie Cutler and Bert Jefferson

7 Helen St James and Don Birnam

8 Barbara Undershaft and Adolphus Cusins

9 Klara Novak and Alfred Kralik

10 Clara Snyder and Marty Pilletti

11 Ilsa Lund Laszlo and Rick Blaine

12 Elaine Harper and Mortimer Brewster

13 Fran Kubelik and C. C. Baxter

14 Trudy Kockenlocker and Norval Jones

15 Eddie Doyle and Terry Malloy

16   Madge Owens and Hal Carter

17   Mary Kate Danaher and Sean Thornton

18   Kathy Selden and Don Lockwood

19   Brigid O'Shaughnessy and Sam Spade (1940)

20   Marie Browning and Harry Morgan

21   Vicki Lester and Norman Maine (1954)

22   Dr Constance Petersen and J. B.

23   Joey Drayton and John Prentice

24   Sarah Brown and Sky Masterson

25   Elaine Robinson and Ben Braddock

26   Pearl Chavez and Lewt McCanles

27   Phyllis Dietrichson and Walter Neff

28   Irena Dubrovna and Oliver Reed

29   Holly Golightly and Paul Varjak

30   Lise Bourvier and Jerry Mulligan

SILENCE PLEASE III (Difficult)

1 When Nazimova in 1921 appeared in CAMILLE, who was her leading man?

2 In 1923, what son of a famous father made his debut in STEPHEN STEPS OUT?

3 In 1926 John Barrymore appeared in DON JUAN, the first film with synchronised music. Who directed it?

4 J. Warren Kerrigan and Lois Wilson starred in 1923 in one of the screen's most historically famous films, a period adventure directed by James Cruze. Name it.

5 In 1921 a fur company named Revillon Freres commissioned Robert J. Flaherty to make a documentary film. Name it.

6 In 1921 FOOLISH WIVES established the reputation of director Erich von Stroheim. Name his first feature in similar vein, made two years earlier.

7 In 1921 Harry C. Myers appeared in a Mark Twain story filmed more than once since, including a Bing Crosby version of 1948. What was it?

8 In 1923 Laurette Taylor, the Broadway stage actress, paid her only visit to Hollywood to film her most famous success. Name it.

9 The first part of Fritz Lang's Niebelungen Saga, released in 1923, is known as SIEGFRIED. Name the second part.

10 In 1927 D. W. Griffith filmed a novel by Marie Corelli. Name it.

11 Name the 1924 Ernst Lubitsch comedy later remade as ONE HOUR WITH YOU.

12 Sergei Eisenstein's first film, made in 1924, concerned industrial unrest. Name it.

13 Who played Al Jolson's mother in THE JAZZ SINGER?

14 In what 1926 film, remade in 1941 as a Dorothy Lamour vehicle, did Gilda Gray star?

15 In 1923 Charles Chaplin directed but did not appear in his only fully serious film, A WOMAN OF PARIS. Who played the title role?

16 What dapper actor played opposite her?

17 Which actor, who played five roles in 1903's THE GREAT TRAIN ROBBERY, went on to make over four hundred films as a leading western star?

18 In 1923 a German crew filmed DRACULA but to avoid payment of literary rights called it . . . what?

19 In 1925, what famous screen cowboy made his last film, TUMBLEWEEDS?

20 In 1918, in what D. W. Griffith film did Noël Coward appear?

SWAN SONGS (Easy)

Whose final appearances were made in the following films?

1 SARATOGA (1937)

2 THE HARDER THEY FALL (1956)

3 THE INN OF THE SIXTH HAPPINESS (1958)

4 THE CARPETBAGGERS (1963)

5 ADVISE AND CONSENT (1962)

6 A FUNNY THING HAPPENED ON THE WAY TO THE FORUM (1967)

7 HE RAN ALL THE WAY (1951)

8 TO BE OR NOT TO BE (1942)

9 THE STORY OF MANKIND (1957)

10 THE NAKED EDGE (1961)

11 PLAYMATES (1942)

12 SHIP OF FOOLS (1965)

13   THE UNHOLY THREE (1930)

14   MONKEYS GO HOME (1966)

15   SATAN NEVER SLEEPS (1962)

16   GUESS WHO'S COMING TO DINNER (1967)

17   CUBAN REBEL GIRLS (1959)

18   SOYLENT GREEN (1973)

19   TWILIGHT OF HONOR (1963)

20   THE PATSY (1964)

21   ONCE MORE WITH FEELING (1960)

22   MALAYA (1950)

23   THE DEFECTOR (1966)

24   THE MATING GAME (1959)

25   NIGHT WATCH (1973)

BALLETOMANIA (Easy)

1   Name MGM's 1948 ballet drama starring Margaret O'Brien . . .

2   . . . and the 1937 French film on which it was based, starring Mia Slavenska

3   In 1946 Viola Essen and Ivan Kirov appeared in a weird and unsuccessful ballet melodrama scripted by Ben Hecht. Name it.

4   What studio made it in the hope of acquiring a little prestige?

5   Who played the leading role of the impresario in THE RED SHOES?

6   In what city did Moira Shearer's suicide take place?

7   In what film did Danny Kaye find himself in the corps de ballet?

8   Name Gene Kelly's ambitious 1954 ballet film whose failure signalled not only a down trend in his own career but the end of MGM's musical heyday.

9   Name the part-cartoon segment which was released separately.

10 Which musical included the GIRL HUNT ballet?

11 What ballet star played a dramatic role in TORN CURTAIN? (She also danced a little.)

12 What former ballet star played dramatic roles in THE MUSIC LOVERS and THE BOY FRIEND?

THE SERVANT PROBLEM (Easy)

Who played the housekeeper in:

1 THE CAT AND THE CANARY (1939)?
2 REBECCA?

Who played the butler in:

3 SHERLOCK HOLMES FACES DEATH?
4 TROUBLE IN PARADISE?
5 THE SERVANT?
6 BUSMAN'S HONEYMOON (HAUNTED HONEY-MOON)?
7 TOVARICH?
8 THE HOUND OF THE BASKERVILLES (1939)?
9 THE OLD DARK HOUSE (1932)?
10 AND THEN THERE WERE NONE (1945)?

Who played the valet in:

11 TOP HAT?
12 THE GHOST BREAKERS?
13 THANK YOU JEEVES?

Who played the maid in:

14 MR BLANDINGS BUILDS HIS DREAM HOUSE?
15 A CHUMP AT OXFORD?

THE STORYTELLERS (Medium)

Whose voice narrated the following films? To help you, another film in which each actor appeared is given in brackets.

1 HOW THE WEST WAS WON (MURDER MAN)

2 TOM JONES (THE KREMLIN LETTER)

3 DUEL IN THE SUN (MAN IN THE SHADOW)

4 THE VIKINGS (A MAN FOR ALL SEASONS)

5 THE PICTURE OF DORIAN GRAY (SUSPICION)

6 KING OF KINGS (TRENT'S LAST CASE)

7 THE WAR OF THE WORLDS (THE WINSLOW BOY)

8 ZULU (THE LAST DAYS OF DOLWYN)

9 DRAGON SEED (MATA HARI)

10 MACKENNA'S GOLD (A MIDSUMMER NIGHT'S DREAM)

11 THE NIGHT THEY RAIDED MINSKY'S (THE PALM BEACH STORY)

12 QUO VADIS (MADAME CURIE)

CHRISTMAS AT THE MOVIES (Easy)

1 In what film did Bing Crosby first sing WHITE CHRISTMAS?

2 In what film did Laurel and Hardy work for Santa Claus?

3 In the 1970 remake, who played villain Barnaby?

4 Who played the Ghost of Christmas Past to Albert Finney's SCROOGE?

5 Who played Scrooge in MGM's 1938 A CHRISTMAS CAROL?

6 Name the film in which Ralph Richardson played an East Anglian parson whose family came home for Christmas.

7 Name the "angels" in WE'RE NO ANGELS. (Three marks)

8 In what film were Kenneth More and James Robertson Justice among those who spent Christmas in a snowy waste?

9 In what 1946 film did Deborah Kerr play a nun who spent Christmas in India?

10 In what 1955 film did astronauts spend Christmas in a space station?

11 In what film did Lee Marvin play one of the three wise men?

12 What prophetic film began with Christmas shopping in 1940?

13 In what film was Christmas spent at Camelot?

14 And in what film was Christmas spent at Chinon?

15 What famous American Christmas comedy, more recently remade for TV, was retitled THE BIG HEART in Britain in 1947?

IT MUST BE LOVE (Easy)

Name the lovers in:

1   LOVE AFFAIR (1939)

2   LOVE STORY

3   LOVE AMONG THE RUINS

4   LOVE ME OR LEAVE ME

5   LOVE LETTERS

6   THE LOVE PARADE

7   LOVE IS NEWS

8   LOVE ME TONIGHT

9   LOVE IS A MANY-SPLENDORED THING

10   LOVE IS A BALL

11   LOVE UNDER FIRE

12   LOVE WITH THE PROPER STRANGER

Poster 15. Name the missing film title.

ANY COLOUR AS LONG AS IT'S BLACK
(Medium)

Some questions about black actors and subjects.

1 What classic film from a novel by Thomas Dixon had its negro roles played by white actors in blackface?

2 In what film did Paul Robeson and Ethel Waters find a coat full of money?

3 In 1933 Robeson starred in a film directed by Dudley Murphy, from what Eugene O'Neill play?

4 Who played what famous story-telling character in what 1947 Disney film?

5 Who was THE WATERMELON MAN?

6 What was remarkable about Sidney Poitier's role in THE BEDFORD INCIDENT?

7 Who played the old negro in danger of lynching in INTRUDER IN THE DUST?

8 Name Bob Hope's man-servant in THE GHOST BREAKERS, and the nickname by which he was previously known.

9 Name the all-black remakes of THE INFORMER, ODD MAN OUT and THE ASPHALT JUNGLE.

10 Fats Waller and Katherine Dunham were two of the guests in what all-star all-black musical of 1942?

11 Who played BLACULA?

12 Name the black pianist in CASABLANCA.

13 Name the three stars of UPTOWN SATURDAY NIGHT, and its sequel.

14 Who won an Academy Award for her role as Mammy in GONE WITH THE WIND?

15 Who in MR BLANDINGS BUILDS HIS DREAM HOUSE coined the slogan "If you ain't eatin' WHAM you ain't eatin' ham"?

16 Who starred in THE AUTOBIOGRAPHY OF MISS JANE PITTMAN?

17 Give the title of King Vidor's all-black drama of 1929.

18 What black actor starred in Ealing's British coal-mining drama of 1937, and what was its title?

19 What was the title of the 1975 TV series starring Teresa Graves as a black policewoman?

20 What black actor, whose real name was Lincoln Perry, was criticised for presenting a caricature black stereotype in such films as STEAMBOAT ROUND THE BEND and THE SUN SHINES BRIGHT?

MINE, ALL MINE (Medium)

After the break-up of the big studios many actors formed their own production companies to avoid the middle men getting the profits. Of what actor's involvement is each of the following company names a tip-off?

1 Dena

2 Santana

3 Jalem

4 Batjac

5 Bryna

6 Curtwel

7 Grandon

8 Malpaso

9 Pennebaker

10 Portland

11 Artanis

And which producers own the following companies?

12 Shamley

13 Rastar

14 Arcola

REMAKES WITH MUSIC (Easy)

The following are all musicals; but their stories were all filmed previously without music. Can you name the straight version in each case?

1   CAROUSEL

2   THE KING AND I

3   MR MUSIC

4   THREE FOR THE SHOW

5   SILK STOCKINGS

6   IN THE GOOD OLD SUMMERTIME

7   STEP LIVELY

8   THE OPPOSITE SEX

9   HIGH SOCIETY

10 SHE'S WORKING HER WAY THROUGH COLLEGE

11 ABOUT FACE

12 A SONG IS BORN

THE CONNECTION (Difficult)

Can you find a connection – it could be an actor, a writer, a theme, anything – between each of the following pairs?

1 THE POWER AND THE GLORY, CITIZEN KANE

2 Olivier in REBECCA, Aherne in JUAREZ

3 Lionel Stander, Jack Carson

4 Dan O'Herlihy, Paul Mantee

5 THE SPIRAL STAIRCASE, MAD WEDNESDAY

6 THE LADY VANISHES, SO LONG AT THE FAIR

7 THE LADY VANISHES, THE SPIRAL STAIRCASE

8 THE INVISIBLE MAN, JOURNEY'S END (two links)

9 PASSAGE TO MARSEILLES, THE LIFE OF EMILE ZOLA

10 THE BISHOP'S WIFE, IT'S A WONDERFUL LIFE

11 James Stewart, Stewart Granger

12 THE LITTLE FOXES, THE GRAPES OF WRATH

13 THE MERRY WIDOW, SHADOW OF A DOUBT

14 SABOTEUR, DARK PASSAGE

15 DR JEKYLL AND MR HYDE (1931), DARK PASSAGE

16 Wallace Beery, Claude Rains

17 THE LAST DAYS OF POMPEII, JOURNEY TO THE CENTER OF THE EARTH

18 SYLVIA SCARLETT, WINGS OF THE MORNING

19 UN CARNET DE BAL, TALES OF MANHATTAN

20 Herbert Marshall in FOREIGN CORRESPONDENT. Leo G. Carroll in SPELLBOUND

21 BWANA DEVIL, THE ROBE

22 KING KONG (1933), THE FRENCH CONNECTION

23 Robert Morley, Peter Finch

24 MY LAST DUCHESS, YOU JUST KILL ME

25 HELLZAPOPPIN, CITIZEN KANE

26 THE SCARLET EMPRESS, LOST HORIZON

27 FOREIGN CORRESPONDENT, FATE IS THE HUNTER

28   Errol Flynn, Robert Shaw

29   THE WIZARD OF OZ, CHARLIE BUBBLES

30   John Howard, Ron Randell

31   FOOTSTEPS IN THE DARK, LADY ON A TRAIN

32   ALL THAT MONEY CAN BUY, ALIAS NICK BEAL

33   REBECCA, DUEL IN THE SUN

34   REBECCA, EDWARD MY SON

35   THE MAN WHO KNEW TOO MUCH (1934), THE SECRET PARTNER

36   TOBACCO ROAD, GOD'S LITTLE ACRE

37   HARVEY, NIGHT OF THE LEPUS

38   THE TALL TARGET, MRS O'MALLEY AND MR MALONE

39   Barry Fitzgerald, Richard Attenborough

40   W. C. Fields, Ralph Richardson

PLAY IT AGAIN ... WITH VARIATIONS (Easy)

If a star and a story are big enough, a film will be bravely and expensively re-shot with the same title as previous versions: no point, for instance, in concealing that what you are doing is DR JEKYLL AND MR HYDE. But sometimes it is thought prudent to remake a film under a different title in case the public memory of the original is not all that affectionate, or perhaps too vivid. Can you name the titles under which these stories were previously made?

1 THE GIFT OF LOVE

2 LET'S DO IT AGAIN

3 RIDING HIGH

4 A POCKETFUL OF MIRACLES

5 STOLEN HOURS

6 LIVING IT UP

7 YOUNG AT HEART

8 YOU'RE NEVER TOO YOUNG

9 YOU CAN'T RUN AWAY FROM IT

10 STORM OVER THE NILE

11 ONE HOUR WITH YOU

12 THAT WAY WITH WOMEN

13   MARK OF THE VAMPIRE

14   A CHILD IS BORN

15   I'D RATHER BE RICH

16   I DIED A THOUSAND TIMES

17   SLEEPING CAR TO TRIESTE

18   MOVE OVER DARLING

19   THE BIRDS AND THE BEES (1956)

20   HOUSE OF WAX

21   SCARED STIFF

22   THE SHAKIEST GUN IN THE WEST

23   SHORT CUT TO HELL

24   UP TIGHT

25   BARRICADE (1950)

26   THE KING'S PIRATE

27   CONGO MAISIE

28   A PLACE IN THE SUN

29   THE CLOWN

30   THE GIRL MOST LIKELY

31   INTERNATIONAL SQUADRON

32   AN AFFAIR TO REMEMBER

33   ADVENTURE ISLAND

34   SUMMER HOLIDAY (1948)

35   THE BADLANDERS

36   SATAN MET A LADY

37   ISTANBUL

38   STOP YOU'RE KILLING ME

39   SINGAPORE WOMAN

40   BETWEEN TWO WORLDS

COPYCATS: SECOND DIVISION (Difficult)

Give the common link between the following, in terms of roles played, themes used, etc. Name the films concerned.

1   Paul Muni, Ann Dvorak, Cary Grant, Frank Lovejoy

2   H. G. Wells, Mary Shelley, Bram Stoker, R. L. Stevenson

3   Agnes Moorehead, Dustin Hoffman, Sam Jaffe, Charles Boyer

4   John Carradine, Berton Churchill, Donald Meek, Thomas Mitchell

5   Vincent Price, Laurence Olivier, Basil Rathbone

6   Gene Kelly, George Sanders, Tyrone Power, Laurence Harvey

7   John Fraser, Laird Cregar, Jack Palance, Ewen Solon

8   Peter Lorre, Charles Laughton, Peter Ustinov

9   James Garner, John Hodiak, Ronald Colman, Gregory Peck

10 Charlie Ruggles, Jack Benny, Arthur Askey, Ray Bolger

11 Rod Steiger, Herbert Lom, Marlon Brando, Kenneth Haigh

12 SCARFACE, THE OUTLAW, VENDETTA, THE FRONT PAGE

13 John Gilbert, Charles Boyer, Melvyn Douglas, Robert Taylor

14 STORMY WEATHER, HALLELUJAH, CABIN IN THE SKY

15 Walter Abel, Don Ameche, Gene Kelly, Michael York

16 STORM WARNING, THE FBI STORY, THE CARDINAL

17 Susan Hayward, Ray Milland, James Cagney, Jack Lemmon

18 THE BIG TRAIL, THE BAT WHISPERS, BILLY THE KID

19 MR MUSIC, COPACABANA, SKIDOO

20 Otis Skinner, Ronald Colman, Howard Keel

21 Melvyn Douglas, Warren William, Gerald Mohr

22 Cedric Hardwicke, Laurence Olivier, Richard Johnson, Peter Finch

23 Rosemary Lane, Loretta Young, Joan Bennett

24 Edmond O'Brien, Clifton Webb, Alec Guinness, Rex Harrison

25 THE FLYING DEUCES, BEAU GESTE, ROGUE'S REGIMENT

26 THE LADY FROM SHANGHAI, STRANGERS ON A TRAIN, THE DANCING MASTERS

27 Jeffrey Hunter, Max Von Sydow, H. B. Warner

28 Fredric March, Jean Gabin, Michael Rennie

29 KIND HEARTS AND CORONETS, DROP DEAD DARLING (ARRIVEDERCI BABY), GET CARTER

30 LILIOM, THE MATCHMAKER, I AM A CAMERA, TOM DICK AND HARRY

31 Seymour Hicks, Alastair Sim, Reginald Owen, Albert Finney

32 WEST OF ZANZIBAR, TELL IT TO THE MARINES, THE PENALTY

33 Ronald Reagan, George Murphy, Shirley Temple

34 PSYCHO, IT HAPPENED ONE NIGHT, A GUIDE FOR THE MARRIED MAN

35 BULLITT, PETULIA, THE MALTESE FALCON

36 LES MISERABLES, THE THIRD MAN, HE WALKED BY NIGHT

37 THE FIEND WHO WALKED THE WEST, BARRICADE (1950), THE UNFAITHFUL

38 A FISTFUL OF DOLLARS, THE MAGNIFICENT SEVEN, THE OUTRAGE

39 THE BLACK ROOM, THE MASQUERADER, THE PRISONER OF ZENDA, WONDER MAN

40 HOG WILD, ME AND MY PAL, NIGHT OWLS, HELPMATES

SOME YEARS LATER (Easy)

Sequels are fairly rare in film business, for the practical reason that it is usually difficult to reassemble casts and/or inspiration. In the seventies however, we had FRENCH CONNECTION II and EXORCIST II and even a sequel to GONE WITH THE WIND. Casting your mind much farther back, to what successful films were the following direct sequels, using at least one continuing cast member in the same character?

1 BY THE LIGHT OF THE SILVERY MOON

2 I'LL BE YOURS

3 THE ROAD BACK

4 BELLES ON THEIR TOES

5 THE RETURN OF FRANK JAMES

6 THEY CALL ME MISTER TIBBS

7 WHERE THE BULLETS FLY

8 FROM RUSSIA WITH LOVE

9 YOU'RE ONLY YOUNG ONCE

10 FOUR WIVES

11 DEMETRIUS AND THE GLADIATORS

FOR THE VERY FIRST TIME IN THE HISTORY OF THE CINEMA (Easy)

Each of the following films is notable for a technical advance which was thought worth advertising at the time. Can you say what?

1 THE BIG TRAIL (1930)

2 BWANA DEVIL

3 THE GLORIOUS ADVENTURE (1921)

4 THE ROBE

5 WHITE CHRISTMAS

6 FANTASIA

7 BECKY SHARP

8 THE TRAIL OF THE LONESOME PINE (1936)

9 THE JAZZ SINGER (1927)

10 LIGHTS OF NEW YORK

11 DON JUAN

12 HOUSE ON HAUNTED HILL

HELL CAME TO TOWN WEARING A BADGE!

Every man and woman was marked...and every second drew each of them closer to their fate!

ALAN **LADD** / DON **MURRAY** / DAN **O'HERLIHY**

DOLORES MICHAELS / BARRY COE

PRODUCED BY SYDNEY BOEHM | DIRECTED BY JAMES B. CLARK | SCREENPLAY BY AARON SPELLING & SYDNEY BOEHM

CINEMASCOPE COLOR by DE LUXE

Poster 16. Name the missing film title.

IT ENDED LIKE THIS (Easy)

Of what films were these the last scenes?

1. A reporter, stabbed some while ago, falls into the camera, dead.
2. Two men walk away from the camera across a darkened airport tarmac.
3. A tramp and a girl walk away from the camera up an empty road towards the hills.
4. An amiable fellow leaves a large gated house and strolls into the sunset while chatting with an apparently invisible friend.
5. A taxi driver claims to be a coffee pot.
6. In a lane near a cemetery, a man and a woman approach each other but pass without speaking.
7. A woman sings in a pot, and four men throw things at her.
8. After a visit to a tobacconist, a man remembers his past life and returns to the woman and the home he most loved.
9. A murderer is crushed under a fairground carousel.
10. In a house on fire, a monogrammed pillow is consumed by the flames.
11. In a studio representation of Venice, two people dance over a bridge.
12. A theatrical producer looks out of a window and in the lonely night street sees a woman catch up with a man who is walking slowly away.
13. A boatman, munching a sandwich, walks into an island house as two people leave.
14. A small boat is being towed into port but the two people in it prefer to be left alone; they let the rope go and sink from sight.

15 A neon sign for Cook's Tours flashes on and off.

16 A soldier is shot dead while reaching for a butterfly.

17 A man sits on a fence, finishes a peach pie, gets out a notebook, studies it carefully, looks up in thought, spots someone in the audience, smiles and points . . .

18 A lone man battling a snowstorm in a mountain land rounds a corner and sees ahead the destination he has long been seeking. Bells begin to ring.

19 An elderly gentleman is ushered to an elevator in which he expects to descend. But his saturnine host assures him that his direction is "up".

20 A wedding car carrying bride and bridegroom drives up a hill away from the camera.

21 A woman changes her mind about joining her lover on a train to Paris and sets off to comfort the wounded admirer she has previously rejected.

22 The hero and heroine joyfully enter a room in which an old lady sits playing a piano.

23 After being threatened with hanging, hero and heroine find themselves unexpectedly waterbound and swimming for shore.

24 The heroine runs happily towards the camera calling: "Stephen!"

25 An ex-schoolmaster staggers back to his former classroom and dies there.

26 An architect finds himself caught up in an endless cycle of recurring dreams about a professional visit to a stranger named Eliot Foley at his home, Pilgrims Farm.

27 An old man calls on a married couple to see their young son, who looks suspiciously like himself. The father looks at the audience and says: "We adopted him . . ."

28   Police take the heroine to an elevator, which begins to descend as the hero walks away.

29   A murderer released from prison suddenly realises he has left his incriminating memoirs inside.

30   A young girl wakes up in bed to find that well-wishers present include her aunt and uncle, three farm-hands and a travelling showman.

LAST LINES (Easy)

At the end of which films were the following lines spoken, and by whom?

1   This is the end, the absolute end!

2   I always wear a bullet-proof vest around the studio.

3   I knew a feller once . . .

4   Hello, everybody. This is Mrs Norman Maine . . .

5   Marry me, Emily, and I'll never look at any other horse.

6   Ah, Roger, this is silly.
     – I know, but I'm sentimental.

7   That's not the northern lights, that's Manderley!

8   Mother of Mercy, is this the end of Rico?

9   Can't nobody wipe us out. Can't nobody lick us. We'll go on forever, pa. We're the people.

10   Louis, I think this is the beginning of a beautiful friendship.

PICTURE QUIZ

1 No marks for guessing THE WIZARD OF OZ. But can you give the
   character name of the dog? Name another film in which the Scarecrow
   (name him) appeared with Judy Garland? Name the wizard — and his
   brother, who also appeared in many films? (Their real name was
   Wupperman, if it helps.) Name the Lion's last film? Say how the Tin Man
   (name him) would have been related to Judy Garland were she still alive?
   Name the author of THE WIZARD OF OZ?

2 Ah yes, a Frankenstein film. But which one? And who is playing the monster? Who are the other two people? And what other famous horror star appears in this film, playing what part?

3 Still on the theme of light disguise, who are these two hippies? What is the film? In what other film did they play man and wife?

4 A scene from a British version of a famous farce. What farce? Who wrote
it? Who is the lady? What other three actors have played the role since
sound? Who is the gentleman on the left? In what 1944 film from a novel
by Louis Golding did he star?

5   Easy. Who is in the tub? What is the film? What actor has the last line?
What is the last line? Alright, one mark for naming the blonde.

6 Ah, not so easy. This is a ghost story. Name the two people shown, and the
female star who is not shown. Name the film, and the author of the original
story.

7 The gent on the left must be familiar. Name him and the film, also the film
in which he played Mr Blore. What role did he play in the 1935 DAVID
COPPERFIELD? The gent on the right has had a forty-year career as a star.
Who is he, and in what film did he direct himself?

8   Who are these actors? What is the film? In what film was the gentleman on
    the left saved by what old lady and what boy from a lynching? In what film
    did the gentleman in the centre make his debut? In what musical did the
    gentleman on the right play the romantic lead?

9   A portrait. Name the star and the film.

10   This should be easy. Who is the actor shown? What is the movie? Who
directed the movie? If this is after, who played before? In what film did this
actor play a college killer?

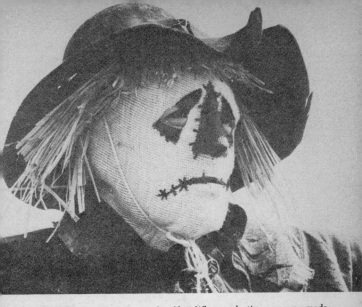

11   Can you deduce who this is, in what film? What production company made
      it? What actors played the role in the two other versions, and what were
      the films called? Who wrote the original novel?

12   Who is he? What film?

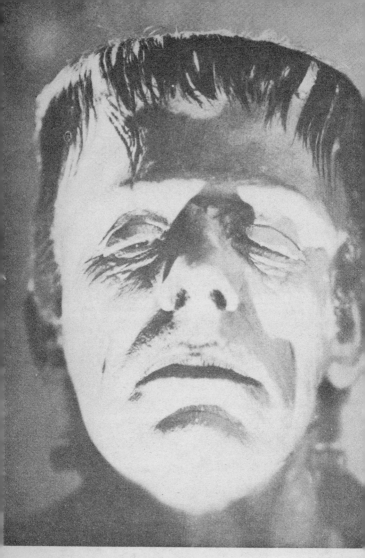

13   Well, let's see if this fools you. Who is he? In which long-running TV series
      did he have a continuing part?

14 Name the four lively gentlemen and the film in which they are appearing,
also the director who made such a comparative mess of it after its highly
successful stage career.

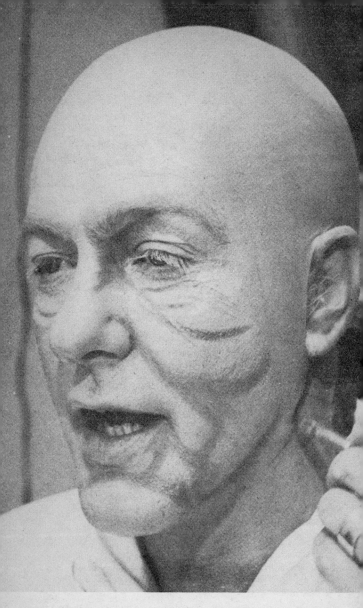

15 A little bit of a cheat, as the make-up isn't complete. We'll tell you that it isn't a horror piece, and see if you can name the actor, the character he plays, and the title.

16 Six well-known faces can be clearly seen in this picture. Who are they, what
    is the film, and who produced it? Who wrote the original story?

17 Naming the actors is almost too easy, but do it. Say also by what names
    the film was known in Britain and in America; and name the young lady
    who made her name in the title role.

18   What a lot of jolly japers! Batman and Robin are obvious, but can you name the actors? And for the others, left to right, please give the actors plus the characters they are portraying.

19   Tricky, this. The four actors at the counter were members of what film family? Can you name them separately?

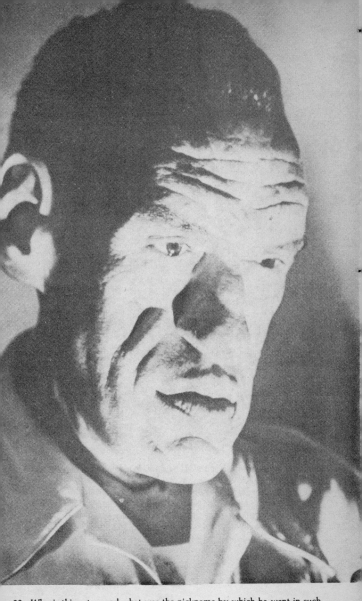

20 Who is this actor, and what was the nickname by which he went in such films as THE PEARL OF DEATH?

21   Three lovely character men. Name them. Which one had the real name
      Guenther Schneider? Name the John Ford film in which the one in the
      middle finally played a really memorable role. In which two films did the
      man on the right play Diamond Jim Brady? Can you possibly name the
      film? Would it help if we said it was directed by James Whale and came
      from a novel called THE HANGOVER MURDERS, or if we murmured the
      stars' names as Robert Young and Constance Cummings?

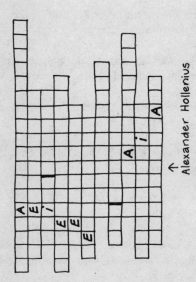

Young lawyer
Max Corkle
Emperor
Medical student
Emperor's wife
Singer
Nazi
Werewolf
Actress
Cellist
Senator

↑
Alexander Hollenius

Laddergram 16

REAL NAME ROMANCE (Medium)

Real instead of assumed names have been used below. Give the stars and the film.

1   Ira Grossel and Ella Geisman were directed by a German in this forgettable piece which also featured Mary Astor.

2   Ruby Stevens and Issur Danielovitch Demsky appeared in this murderous saga which began with the violent end of the heroine's aunt.

3   Maria Magdalena Von Losch meets Reginald Truscott-Jones in a saga of European wanderings.

4   Virginia Katherine McMath and Archibald Leach find fun and romance while eluding the Nazis.

5   Tula Finklea and Frederick Austerlitz in a tale of Russian–American understanding.

6   Jane Peters and Benny Kubelsky in a black comedy about Europe under Nazi rule.

7   Constance Keane and Frederick McIntyre Bickel in a ghost story with the gallic touch.

8   Edythe Marrener was actually the victim of Reginald Carey in this wordy, sometimes witty updating of a seventeenth-century play.

9   Spangler Arlington Brough and Harlean Carpenter in a light comedy about a bailiff in the house.

10 Lucille La Sueur and Jules Garfinkel in a tragic musical romance from a novel by Fannie Hurst.

11 Claire Weinlinger and Marion Michael Morison find romance in the old west.

12 Gladys Greene and Frank Cooper in a story originally called OPERA HAT.

13 Sarah Jane Fulks and Roy Scherer in a twice-filmed novel by Lloyd C. Douglas.

14 James Stewart and Margarita Carmen Cansino in a story from the Old Testament.

THE PLOT THICKENS (Easy)

Can you recognise these well-known films from the following accurate but rather po-faced descriptions of their plots?

1 A journalist sets out to interview Susan Alexander, followed by Messrs Bernstein, Leland and Raymond, in his search for the truth about a tycoon recently deceased.

2 Mr and Mrs Charles Condomine invite to dinner Dr and Mrs Bradman plus one other guest who inadvertently brings along someone quite unexpected and unwanted.

3 Fred Blythe and Charlie Wilder are among the people who turn up at an old house for the reading of a will by Lawyer Crosby.

4 Johnny Jones is told by his editor to change his name to Huntley Haverstock and head for London.

5 Peter Warne spots a runaway heiress at a bus station.

6 Somewhere in Europe, Miss Froy is among several English people waiting for a train to take them home.

7 As schoolchildren, Randy Monaghan, Parris Mitchell, Cassandra Tower and Drake McHugh form a friendship which in adult life has some tragic repercussions.

8 George Bailey tries to commit suicide but is dissuaded by an angel.

9 In New York's Plaza Hotel, Roger Thornhill is mistaken for someone else.

10 Roger Penderel and Philip Waverton, among others, are stranded at night in the Welsh hills during a storm.

11 Wally Cook is sent by his editor to a Vermont village to cover the story of a dying girl.

12 Marion Crane and her boy friend enjoy some lunchtime lovemaking, after which events suddenly send her on a fatal drive.

13 A man whose real name is Charles Ranier, but becomes temporarily known as Smitty, escapes from a mental institution in the English Midlands.

14 In San Francisco, a detective named Miles Archer is shot during his first night on what seems to be a simple case.

15 Monte Beragon is murdered in his beach house by one of two women.

TRIPLE TROUBLE II (Medium)

The three stars linked played the same role in different versions of the same story, not always under the same title. Name the films in each case.

1 Mae Clarke, Vivien Leigh, Leslie Caron

2 John Boles, Dennis Morgan, Gordon Macrae

3 Ruth Chatterton, Gladys George, Lana Turner

4 Janet Gaynor, Shirley Temple, Leslie Caron

5 John Gilbert, Fredric March, Kieron Moore

6 Edward G. Robinson, Raymond Massey, Barry Sullivan

7 Theda Bara, Claudette Colbert, Elizabeth Taylor

8 Lewis Stone, Ronald Colman, Stewart Granger

9 Humphrey Bogart, John Garfield, Audie Murphy

10 Maurice Chevalier, Don Ameche, Danny Kaye

11 Lon Chaney, Claude Rains, Herbert Lom

12 Norma Talmadge, Norma Shearer, Jeanette MacDonald

13 Colleen Moore, Barbara Stanwyck, Jane Wyman

14 Richard Dix, Gene Raymond, Philip Terry

15 Mary Pickford, Marian Nixon, Shirley Temple

16 Bette Davis, Eleanor Parker, Kim Novak

17 Glenn Hunter, Stuart Erwin, Red Skelton

18 Warner Baxter, Alan Ladd, Robert Redford

19 Wallace Reid, Bob Hope, Dean Martin

20 Adolphe Menjou, Cary Grant, Walter Matthau

21 Mary Philbin, Susanna Foster, Heather Sears

22 Harry Myers, Will Rogers, Bing Crosby

23 Jack Buchanan, Dennis O'Keefe, Jack Watling

24 Irene Dunne, Margaret Sullavan, Susan Hayward

25 Betty Compson, Marlene Dietrich, Anne Baxter

26 Lionel Barrymore, Walter Huston, Jose Ferrer

CLOSING TEST PAPER (Difficult)

1   What is the obvious link between these three films of the early fifties: THOSE REDHEADS FROM SEATTLE, GUN FURY, SANGAREE?

2   Who played Puck in the 1935 version of A MID-SUMMER NIGHT'S DREAM?

3   Name the novel by Jerome Weidman on which was based the 1951 film now known variously as ONLY THE BEST (American TV) and THIS IS MY AFFAIR (GB)?

4   In which film did Faye Dunaway and Steve McQueen play chess?

5   And in which film did Boris Karloff and Bela Lugosi play chess?

6   And in which film did Nigel Green and Richard Johnson play chess with outsize pieces?

7   Finally on this topic, in what film did the floor-stones of the hall of an old mansion, when viewed as a chess-board, help towards finding long lost treasure?

8   The same title was used for a film made in 1942 with Brian Donlevy, a quite different film in 1956 with Edward G. Robinson, and in 1956 a Hammer horror mystery with Moira Redmond. What was the title?

9   What Harold Lloyd film is in danger of being confused with one by Luis Bunuel?

10 What came between IN THE HEAT OF THE NIGHT and THE ORGANIZATION?

11 Bette Davis was JEZEBEL but what female star in 1953 appeared in SINS OF JEZEBEL?

12 The three dancing male leads of IT'S ALWAYS FAIR WEATHER were Gene Kelly, Dan Dailey and . . . ?

13 John Carradine in 1943 and Anton Diffring in 1976 played the same real-life role. Who did they portray, and name the two films.

14 What Edgar Wallace play was filmed by Paramount in 1938 as DANGEROUS TO KNOW, starring Akim Tamiroff and Anna May Wong?

15 What book by J. Edgar Hoover provided the substance for four Paramount second features in 1938–40, vaguely based on real public enemies of the thirties?

16 Name the four films.

17 Claude Rains was THE INVISIBLE MAN but who played the lead in THE INVISIBLE MAN RETURNS?

18 And who was the villain of that film?

19 In FOUR DAUGHTERS in 1938 Claude Rains played the father. Who did so in the 1955 remake called YOUNG AT HEART?

20 Name the two direct sequels to FOUR DAUGHTERS.

21 Name also the semi-sequel made in 1939 with virtually the same cast playing different characters in very much the same atmosphere.

22 Name the 1939 film about lady pilots, starring Alice Faye, Constance Bennett and Nancy Kelly.

23 The Massachusetts witch trials of 1692, treated famously in LES SORCIERES DE SALEM, were also the subject of a surprisingly serious Paramount film of 1937. Name it and its two stars.

24 A Warren Beatty film, made as THE PRESBY-TERIAN CHURCH WAGER, had its title changed to . . .

25 An American writer-director whose career suffered from the McCarthy witch hunt is perhaps best known for a 1948 film about the numbers racket. Name him, the film and its star.

26 Two more marks if you can name the original novel and author.

27 A three-hour TV movie made in 1976 treated the 1954 court case in which a Cleveland osteopath was accused of murdering his wife. Name film and star.

28 An even longer TV movie in 1974 dramatised Loen Uris' book QB VII. Name the two male leads.

29 Who played the judge?

30 Who in the 1971 TV movie GOODBYE RAGGEDY ANN played a Hollywood starlet driven to the brink of suicide?

31 A 1972 TV movie called HAUNTS OF THE VERY RICH was a partial and unofficial remake of a 1924 play by Sutton Vane which was filmed in 1931 with Leslie Howard. Name it.

32 The 1944 remake starring Paul Henried and Eleanor Parker had a different title. What was it?

33 Who played the Examiner?

34 The gorilla was a fairly innocent party in 1954's GORILLA AT LARGE. So whodunit?

35 Who played Saladin in the 1953 KING RICHARD AND THE CRUSADERS?

36 HUMAN DESIRE (1950) was an American remake (more or less) of what 1938 French film?

37 Who compered in the 1950 version of LA RONDE?

38 Who directed it?

39 What 1934 period piece now appears on American TV as FORBIDDEN ALLIANCE?

40 Why?

41 For the same reason the 1934 version of THE MERRY WIDOW is shown on TV as . . . ?

42 Who were the co-stars of the 1952 version?

43 John Gregory Dunne wrote a book called THE STUDIO. What studio?

44 Give the title and author of the famous book about the making of THE RED BADGE OF COURAGE.

45 What was remarkable about Claude Rains' film debut?

46 What classic film makes heroes of the Ku Klux Klan?

47 What did Arthur Housman and Jack Norton have in common?

48 For what contemporary historical role, which he played many times, was Robert Watson famous?

49 One might ask the same of Martin Kosleck.

50 What British leading man more or less forsook acting to be Cecil B. De Mille's right hand and associate producer?

51 What part did he play in MRS MINIVER?

52 What elderly British gentleman was the leading character, though not the top billed star, of MISTER 880 and APARTMENT FOR PEGGY?

53 What famous star of the fifties was seen briefly as a soda jerk in HAS ANYBODY SEEN MY GAL?

54 What novel by Hervey Allan was filmed in 1936 and helped Gale Sondergaard win an Academy Award as best supporting actress?

55 What star of the forties is to be glimpsed as a pipe-smoking reporter towards the end of CITIZEN KANE?

56 What has THE KING AND THE CHORUS GIRL to do with DOUBLE DYNAMITE?

57 Novelist Hugh Walpole played what role in what Hollywood film in 1935?

58 In what film did Humphrey Bogart play a murderer, hounded into giving himself away by Sidney Green-street's clever ruses?

59 Under what name did Arthur Stanley Jefferson, of Ulverston, Lancashire, England, become famous when he went to Hollywood?

60 In what film did Colonel Strasser and Captain Renault appear, and who played them?

61 In what semi-horror film did Elspeth Dudgeon play a gentleman?

62 What distinction was given in the fifties to Adeline de Walt Reynolds?

63 Who held the same distinction in 1976, and in what film did she co-star?

64 Who thought he could imitate the cry of a loon in BRINGING UP BABY?

65 What continuing star role was played by a fellow named Pal?

66 Who played Soames Forsythe in THAT FORSYTHE WOMAN?

67 What is the connection between Melville Crossman and Mark Canfield?

68 What famous studio has a motto meaning "art for art's sake"?

69 In what film did James Mason, uncredited, play an Arab beggar?

70 Why was Anthony Quinn a fairly natural choice to direct De Mille's last film THE BUCCANEER when CB wasn't up to it?

71 In what film did Will Hay play a magistrate and John Mills his son?

72 In SORROWFUL JONES (1949) Mary Jane Saunders played an orphan girl involved with racetrack gangsters and Bob Hope. The 1934 version of the same story starred Shirley Temple and was called . . . ?

73 In what film did Shirley Temple co-star with Carole Lombard and Gary Cooper?

74 Who directed it?

75 Laird Cregar is said to have died from losing weight to play the lead in what film?

76 In what film did he play a character called Stephen Spettigue, and who played the title role?

77 In what 1973 TV movie did Tom Courtenay play a young priest dying in a remote Canadian village?

78 THE MOON AND SIXPENCE (1942) was based on a novel by . . . ?

79 On the life of what famous artist is it said to be based?

80 Who played the artist whose wife George Sanders steals?

81 And who played the wife?

82 Name the MR BELVEDERE sequels to the 1948 SITTING PRETTY.

83 In what film did Lena Horne and Eddie Anderson sing CONSEQUENCE?

84 What film made Walter Huston's rendering of SEPTEMBER SONG popular?

85 In what film did Ray Bolger sing ONCE IN LOVE WITH AMY?

86 Of what film did the British Board of Film Censors say many years ago: "It has no apparent meaning. If there is a meaning it is doubtless objectionable."

87 In MR BLANDINGS BUILDS HIS DREAM HOUSE, who played the helpful but bewildered architect Mr Simms?

88 Who played Frollo in the Charles Laughton version of THE HUNCHBACK OF NOTRE DAME?

89 Who directed it?

90 With what TV project do you connect Nick Nolte and Peter Strauss?

91 Who played Dracula in THE RETURN OF DRACULA?

92 Name the 1933 comedy about a slightly pixilated family; it was said to mark the beginning of the crazy comedy cycle, and starred Claudette Colbert and Mary Boland.

93 A 1968 comedy based on a novel by Charles Webb was a great commercial success. Name it.

94 Who played Mr Jordan in HERE COMES MR JORDAN?

95 A 1974 TV film called IN TANDEM led to a two-season series called . . . ?

96 Name the two stars.

97 Who played the American who tried to educate a Greek prostitute in NEVER ON SUNDAY?

98 Will Hay, comedy star of OH MR PORTER and ASK A POLICEMAN, had two regular stooges. Name them.

99 In 1941 they appeared in a revamping of OH MR PORTER called BACK ROOM BOY. Who was the star?

100 Who in 1932 directed LOVE ME TONIGHT?

101 What director made THE COOL MIKADO, LAWMAN and WON TON TON, THE DOG WHO SAVED HOLLYWOOD?

102 Of what MYSTERY MOVIE TV segments were these the pilots? a) ONCE UPON A DEAD MAN b) RANSOM FOR A DEAD MAN c) SAY HELLO TO A DEAD MAN d) THE BIG RIP-OFF e) WHO KILLED MISS USA? f) DETOUR TO NOWHERE

103 Name the comedy which put Cary Grant and Tony Curtis in a submarine.

104 And the comedy which put Cary Grant and Ann Sheridan on a motor bike?

105 In which musical did we hear the songs STEAM HEAT, I'M NOT AT ALL IN LOVE and HERNANDO'S HIDEAWAY?

106 Name the leading man.

107 What much-filmed best seller was written by Grace Metalious?

108 And what earlier small-town saga, also filmed and later made the basis of a TV series, was written by Henry Bellamann?

109 In what film did George Sanders wear women's clothes?

110 Who was the common star of THE PHANTOM CREEPS (1939) and THE APE MAN (1943)?

111 Name the 1944 film in which Cary Grant promoted a dancing caterpillar?

112 Who played the boy owner of the catterpillar?

113 Name the lady who in 1932 was billed above Jean Harlow in PLATINUM BLONDE.

114 The hero of PLATINUM BLONDE gave an excellent performance but died soon after it was finished. Name him.

115 Who directed the 1967 film PLANET OF THE APES?

116 What 1930 Cecil B. De Mille film has for its climax a disaster in an airship?

117 What episodic 1942 film was linked by a tail-coat?

118 And which 1943 ditto by the ramblings of a club bore?

119 The last two films had the same director. Name him.

120 What musical was based on a Richard Bissell novel called 7½ CENTS?

121 What actor played Dr Watson to the Sherlock Holmes of Arthur Wontner?

122 What actor played Inspector Lestrade in six of the films in which Basil Rathbone played Sherlock Holmes?

123 Name the Rathbone/Holmes film based on the original Conan Doyle story THE SIX NAPOLEONS.

124 Who played Moriarty in THE ADVENTURES OF SHERLOCK HOLMES?

125 And who in THE WOMAN IN GREEN?

126 Who played in the 1931 versions of both FRANKEN-
STEIN and DRACULA, in the former as Frankenstein's elderly mentor and in the latter as Van Helsing?

127 Name also the actor who played the hunchback assistant
in FRANKENSTEIN and Jonathan Harker in
DRACULA.

128 What was the 1932 horror movie of circus life made
by Tod Browning, which MGM disowned after seeing
it?

129 Who played Katharine Hepburn's sister in THE
PHILADELPHIA STORY?

130 Who in 1942 played THE YOUNG MR PITT?

131 In the same film, who played Charles James Fox?

132 In 1938, who played opposite Joan Crawford in
MANNEQUIN?

133 Who was the director of LES ENFANTS DU
PARADIS?

134 With what branch of cinema art do you associate
Joseph H. August?

135 And Constantin Bakaleinikoff?

136 Name the unseen zither player in THE THIRD MAN.

137 What famous comedy-thriller was filmed three times,
starring Guy Newall, Jack Hulbert, and Arthur Askey?

138 Name the Martin and Lewis remake of THE GHOST
BREAKERS.

139 Who should have played the Raymond Massey part in
ARSENIC AND OLD LACE?

140 In what film were Lamberto Maggiorani and Enzo
Staiola the leading players?

141 A 1932 Warren William film called THE MOUTH-
    PIECE was twice remade, once with George Brent
    and once with Edward G. Robinson. Name the two
    films.

142 Who played Judas in the 1927 KING OF KINGS?

143 Who played Hamlet in the 1964 Russian version?

144 A 1936 Al Jolson film was known in Great Britain
    as CASINO DE PAREE. Give the American title and
    say who co-starred.

145 THE SPOILERS has been filmed five times. Who
    wrote the novel?

146 Who took over in 1955 Marlene Dietrich's role of the
    saloon entertainer Cherry Malotte?

147 Name the Roman epic which Alexander Korda began
    in 1937 but never finished.

148 What continuing role did Tom Conway take over
    from George Sanders?

149 Who provided the voices for cartoon characters Speedy
    Gonzales, Bugs Bunny and Sylvester (among others)?

150 In the films of the same names, what are the Blue
    Gardenia, the Blue Angel and the Blue Dahlia?

151 Who played Poppea in THE SIGN OF THE CROSS?

152 In what liquid did she allegedly take her bath?

153 Who played Androcles in ANDROCLES AND THE
    LION?

154 And who played Petronius in the 1951 QUO VADIS?

155 What does QUO VADIS mean?

156 What does HATARI mean?

157 What singing star, whose story was filmed in 1955, appeared in ROMAN SCANDALS with Eddie Cantor?

158 Name the 1955 film.

159 How many stories were there in THE NAKED CITY (1948), according to the closing voice-over? (It will be more now.)

160 Who are The Archers? What was their function?

161 In 1950 David Lean directed a period crime story about a famous unsolved case. Whose case, and who played the title role?

162 Margaret Lockwood and James Mason provided the villainous element in THE MAN IN GREY. Who completed the stellar quartet?

163 What horror film produced – and some say directed – by Howard Hawks took place north of the Arctic Circle?

164 Who played CITIZEN KANE's second wife?

165 And who played his butler?

166 What was the name of his castle?

167 In JOURNEY INTO FEAR Orson Welles played the head of the Turkish police. Name him.

168 Who played Esmeralda to Lon Chaney's HUNCHBACK OF NOTRE DAME?

169 And to Charles Laughton's?

170 And to Anthony Quinn's?

171 In THE WIZARD OF OZ, who played the Witch of the East?

:72 What is the connection between that film and one by John Boorman?

173 Name the film from a novel by John O'Hara in which Suzanne Pleshette played a nymphomaniac.

174 STORM OVER THE NILE was a 1956 remake of what famous story filmed in 1929 and 1939?

175 Who wrote the novel?

176 Who played Pa Joad in THE GRAPES OF WRATH?

177 Which studio made it?

178 To what film was this tagline applied? "He's just as funny as his old man was fierce."

179 Who played Ferrari the black marketeer of CASA-BLANCA?

180 Who played Ugarte?

181 In what film did James Mason play the evil Sir Brack?

182 Who co-starred with Robert Donat in THE COUNT OF MONTE CRISTO?

183 In 1951 Donat appeared as a cinema pioneer in a biopic called THE MAGIC BOX. Who was the pioneer?

184 Who played the policeman brought off the street to see the first moving pictures?

185 Who is Eddie Egan?

186 Who is Van Nest Polglase?

187 Who is Edith Head?

188 What does Lawrence Tierney have in common with Warren Oates?

189 Who directed THE KING AND I, CAN CAN and SNOW WHITE AND THE THREE STOOGES?

190 To what producer-director, who died in 1963, was Maureen O'Sullivan married?

191 In what film did she play Jane Bennet?

192 What in 1914 did Phyllis Haver, Marie Prevost and Ruth Taylor have in common?

193 Who was the female star of ROSALIE and I DOOD IT?

194 Name the 1939 film in which John Barrymore was directed by Garson Kanin.

195 Which famous director, early in his career, made LABURNHAM GROVE, MIDSHIPMAN EASY and A GIRL MUST LIVE?

196 Who played Lady Catherine de Burgh in PRIDE AND PREJUDICE?

197 Who played the monster in THE GHOST OF FRANKENSTEIN?

198 And in HOUSE OF FRANKENSTEIN?

199 In the above picture, who played DRACULA?

200 Who played Nurse Peggotty in DAVID COPPER-FIELD (1935)?

201 She married Barkis the coachman, played by who?

202 Who played Jack Holt's mother in SAN FRAN-CISCO?

203 Who played Carlotta Vance in DINNER AT EIGHT?

204 Who were the stars of HALF SHOT AT SUNRISE, MUMMY'S BOYS and CRACKED NUTS?

205 Who played Granny in GRANNY GET YOUR GUN?

206 What was curious about the script of this film?

207 Which silent film directed by Erich von Stroheim had its climax in Death Valley?

208 Name the two male leads.

213

209 Name the little-seen film starring Rod Steiger, Susannah York, Don Murray and George Grizzard.

210 What famous star was seen as a dancer in the 1935 DANTE'S INFERNO?

211 In what city was WHAT'S UP DOC shot?

212 Of what film was a character named Charlie Allnutt the hero?

213 In what film did Bob Hope perform with a penguin?

214 In what film was a director asked to make ANTS IN YOUR PANTS OF 1941? (He preferred to make O BROTHER WHERE ART THOU.)

215 Who said, in what film, "Your wife is safe with Tonetti; he prefers spaghetti"?

216 In what film did H. B. Warner play Chang?

217 In what film was Private Ratskywatsky much talked of though he never appeared?

218 Who played Cardinal Richelieu in Richard Lester's THE THREE MUSKETEERS?

219 And in the Ritz Brothers version of 1939?

220 Who directed the 1945 version of AND THEN THERE WERE NONE?

221 Who directed Humphrey Bogart in SAHARA?

222 Who played Watson in the 1922 SHERLOCK HOLMES?

223 Philip Barry wrote the play THE PHILADELPHIA STORY. Who wrote the film script?

224 What have Charles Ruggles, Arthur Askey, Jack Benny and Ray Bolger in common (apart from all being very funny fellows)?

225 Of what film was WEEKEND AT THE WALDORF (1945) a revised remake?

226 In THE BULLFIGHTERS Laurel and Hardy did a breaking eggs routine, first performed by them and Lupe Velez in what film?

227 In what film did Grusinskaya appear, played by whom?

228 In what film did Cary Grant take a shower fully clothed?

229 In 1948 the first 'cold war' film was the story of Igor Gouzenko. It was called . . . ?

230 Who in 1971 directed THE GARDEN OF THE FINZI-CONTINIS?

231 With whom did Laurel and Hardy have their tit-for-tat wrecking war in BIG BUSINESS?

232 And in BACON GRABBERS?

233 And in TIT FOR TAT?

234 Who played Dr Christian in the series put out by RKO between 1938 and 1941?

235 Who was the director of DOCKS OF NEW YORK, THUNDERBOLT and SERGEANT MADDEN?

236 What famous old-timers starred in a 1972 TV movie called THE CROOKED HEARTS? (Three points for getting all three.)

237 What did Maurice Chevalier originate that Don Ameche and Danny Kaye took over?

238 Who directed the 1921 version of THE FOUR HORSEMEN OF THE APOCALYPSE?

239 Who played the would-be suicide in FOURTEEN HOURS (1951)?

240 In what film did Marlene Dietrich co-star with Charles Boyer?

241 Who said this? "I don't care if he is a walrus. I like him. I like him."

242 What famous film was adapted from a book called PERSONAL HISTORY by Vincent Shehan?

243 Who played Jolson's mentor, later partner and manager in THE JOLSON STORY?

244 Name the actress who played mother in the Hardy family series.

245 What actor *first* played Judge Hardy?

246 Liza Minnelli played Sally Bowles in CABARET; but what actress, discovered by Otto Preminger for EXODUS, first played the role on Broadway?

247 Who played uncredited bit parts in THE MALTESE FALCON and IN THIS OUR LIFE?

248 Who were Flagg and Quirt in the original silent WHAT PRICE GLORY?

249 Who starred in THE SCOUNDREL, written and directed in 1935 by Ben Hecht and Charles MacArthur?

250 Who played Hildy Johnson in the 1930 version of THE FRONT PAGE?

251 How many times has JANE EYRE been filmed since sound?

252 Name the actresses who played the title role in these versions.

253 What connection can you make between Mary Kornmann, Joe Cobb, Mickey Daniels and Jackie Condon?

254 One of Andy Hardy's girl-friends turned up again in 1972 in THEY ONLY KILL THEIR MASTERS. Who was she?

255 Who was Anton Grot?

256 Who played the monster in the immensely long TV movie of 1972: FRANKENSTEIN, THE TRUE STORY?

257 THE THING FROM ANOTHER WORLD became the star of what long-running TV series?

258 Peter Falk is Columbo and Dennis Weaver is McCloud; but who played Faraday of FARADAY AND COMPANY?

259 And who were THE SNOOP SISTERS?

260 What famous Hollywood star of the forties played the victim in their first episode?

261 Who played the hero of the 1922 version of THE PRISONER OF ZENDA and the Cardinal in the 1952 version?

262 Who played Rupert of Hentzau in 1922; 1937; and 1952?

263 In which film did Groucho make the following utterances? To the remark: "This shall be a gala day for you": "Well, a gal a day is enough for me. I don't think I could manage any more."

264 In which film did W. C. Fields play Egbert Souse, pronounced sue-say?

265 Is it true that Sig Rumann suffered at Groucho Marx's hands in A DAY AT THE RACES, A NIGHT IN CASABLANCA and THE BIG STORE?

266 In which film did James Stewart play Wyatt Earp?

267 For what film was the song ISN'T IT ROMANTIC written?

268 Who directed HIGH NOON?

269 Messrs Allen, Flanagan, Knox, Gold, Naughton and Nervo were collectively known as what?

270 Name two of their films.

271 Who played Douglas Bader in what film?

272 What 1924 film starred Wallace Beery and had monsters created by Willis O'Brien?

273 What had Mary Gordon to do with the Basil Rathbone/ Sherlock Holmes films?

274 Who had the last line in SOME LIKE IT HOT? (The 1959 film.)

275 Who played Uncle Matt and Lord Epping, in what series?

276 What was the name of Popeye's girl-friend?

277 What producer-director was responsible for HOMI-CIDAL, THE HOUSE ON HAUNTED HILL and THE TINGLER?

278 What famous film was based on a novel called GLORY FOR ME by Mackinlay Kantor?

279 Who was the common star of THE MUMMY'S TOMB, BOWERY TO BROADWAY, THE CLIMAX and THE MAD GHOUL?

280 Who was Hans Dreier?

SCORECARD

	Possible Score	Your Score	Difficult Medium or Easy
OPENING TEST PAPER	275	......	E
THE OLD SCHOOLHOUSE DOOR	16	......	E
WORLD WAR TWO	21	......	M
BILLY THE KID	10	......	M
THE WARNERS DO IT AGAIN	25	......	D
THE TELEHEROES	26	......	E
IN TWO WORDS, IM POSSIBLE	16	......	M
ALFRED HITCHCOCK PRESENTS	21	......	E
OSCAR, I LOVE YOU	26	......	E
SILENCE PLEASE I	20	......	M
COPYCATS: FIRST DIVISION	121	......	D
IT STARTED THIS WAY	25	......	E
TUT, TUT	20	......	E
FLASHBACK	15	......	E
THEY WENT TO THE MOVIES	12	......	M
THEY SUFFERED A SEA CHANGE I	20	......	M
UP TO DATE	29	......	E
REMAKE ROLES	76	......	E
THE VERY MAN	30	......	E
NO SUB-TITLES REQUIRED	24	......	M
WHAT'S IN A NAME?	26	......	M
WHEN DISASTER STRUCK	40	......	E
BIG JOHN	16	......	E
FROM THE ORIGINAL PLAY	24	......	M
DUCHESS OF HOLLYWOOD	18	......	E

A GOOD CAST IS WORTH REPEATING	50	M
BLESS THESE HOUSES	10	E
THE ADVENTURES OF . . .WHO?	20	E
MATCHED PAIRS	40	M
FLYNN OF BURMA	15	E
EGO	15	M
WOMEN!	20	E
BETTER KNOWN AS	8	E
THE FILM AND THE FACE	50	M
NOT SO FUNNY	20	E
THE MURDERER IS IN THIS ROOM	25	M
FREDERIC IS COMPOSING TONIGHT	54	E
OH, JOHNNY, OH	10	E
MORE THAN ONE TALENT	35	M
THEY SUFFERED A SEA CHANGE II	20	M
DEAR MR GABLE	21	E
THE TOPIC IS BIOPICS	60	M
SILENCE PLEASE II	21	D
COLOURS OF THE RAINBOW	31	E
DEBUTANTES	30	D
UNLIKELY BEHAVIOUR	30	M
HUMBLE BEGINNINGS	24	E
OLD NICK	12	E
FATEFUL MEETINGS	36	M
YOU DIRTY RAT	15	E

WHO NEEDS *TWO* STARS?	50	...... M
TRIPLE TROUBLE I	14	...... E
THE FAMILY HOUR	54	...... D
MORE STARS THAN THERE ARE IN THE SKY	10	...... E
FROM THE ORIGINAL NOVEL	25	...... E
WORLD GAZETTEER	25	...... E
ANATOMY	25	...... E
BIOPICS AGAIN	90	...... E
ACTORS IN COMMON	60	...... D
NUMBERS	30	...... M
SUCH COMMON WORDS	25	...... E
FROM THE ORIGINAL STORY	22	...... M
COMEBACKS	25	...... M
HEROINES AND HEROES	90	...... M
SILENCE PLEASE III	20	...... D
SWAN SONGS	25	...... E
BALLETOMANIA	12	...... E
THE SERVANT PROBLEM	15	...... E
THE STORYTELLERS	12	...... M
CHRISTMAS AT THE MOVIES	17	...... E
IT MUST BE LOVE	24	...... E
ANY COLOUR AS LONG AS IT'S BLACK	27	...... M
MINE, ALL MINE	14	...... M
REMAKES WITH MUSIC	12	...... E
THE CONNECTION	41	...... D
PLAY IT AGAIN, WITH VARIATIONS	40	...... E

COPYCATS: SECOND DIVISION	103	D
SOME YEARS LATER	11	E
FOR THE VERY FIRST TIME	12	E
IT ENDED LIKE THIS	30	E
LAST LINES	21	E
REAL NAME ROMANCE	42	M
THE PLOT THICKENS	15	E
TRIPLE TROUBLE II	48	M
CLOSING TEST PAPER	328	D
PICTURE QUIZ	119	M
16 LADDERGRAMS	398	D
POSTER TITLES	16	M
	3571	

NB. It will be noted that there are more than the promised three thousand five hundred questions. The extra 75 are to give you leeway for all those occasions when you really knew the answer all the time, but just couldn't bring it to mind.

THE ANSWERS

Score one point for every square you can *honestly* tick as an indication that you really knew the answer. The answers to the picture quiz are at the end of this section.

OPENING TEST PAPER

1 Paris ☐ 2 John Ford ☐ 3 CONQUEST (GB: MARIE WALEWSKA) ☐ 4 THE COVERED WAGON ☐ 5 BROKEN BLOSSOMS ☐ 6 Alfred Hitchcock ☐ 7 Alexander Korda ☐ 8 Herman J. Mankiewicz ☐ 9 Jack Oakie ☐ 10 FANTASIA ☐ 11 THE PRIDE OF THE YANKEES ☐ 12 David Lean ☐ 13 UTOPIA ☐ 14 MIRACLE IN MILAN ☐ 15 Sidney Howard ☐ was credited, though many others contributed, including the producer, David O Selznick 16 THE MUMMY ☐, MAD LOVE ☐ 17 Sergei Eisenstein ☐ 18 Boris Karloff ☐ 19 THE MUSIC BOX ☐ 20 Werner Krauss ☐ 21 Abbott and Costello ☐ 22 SMILES OF A SUMMER NIGHT ☐ 23 Leslie Banks ☐ 24 Humphrey Jennings ☐ 25 THE ROAD BACK ☐ 26 Anton Walbrook ☐ 27 Noël Coward ☐ 28 Horace Horsecollar ☐ 29 FORBIDDEN PARADISE ☐ 30 John Wayne ☐ 31 Grumpy ☐ Doc ☐ 32 Stanley Cortez ☐ 33 MONSIEUR VERDOUX ☐ 34 UN CARNET DE BAL ☐ 35 LYDIA ☐ Merle Oberon ☐ 36 KIND HEARTS AND CORONETS ☐ 37 JOUR DE FETE ☐ 38 CARRY ON SERGEANT ☐ 39 ROOM SERVICE ☐ 40 STEP LIVELY ☐ 41 William S. Hart ☐ 42 Milos Forman ☐ 43 IT HAPPENED ONE NIGHT ☐ 44 SCARFACE ☐ 45 Mickey Rooney ☐ 46 Andre Morell ☐ 47 Anton Walbrook ☐ 48 Howard Hawks ☐ 49 Anna Neagle ☐ 50 Irving Berlin ☐ 51 Nelson Eddy ☐ Jeanette MacDonald ☐ 52 SILK STOCKINGS, a musical reprise of NINOTCHKA ☐ 53 FURY ☐ 54 United Productions of America, or UPA ☐ 55 Alexander Knox ☐ 56 MONKEY BUSINESS ☐

57 DRIFTERS ☐ 58 Rene Clair ☐ 59 THE EAGLE ☐ 60 Compton Mackenzie ☐ 61 David Niven ☐ 62 THE SMALL BACK ROOM ☐ 63 SHADOW OF A DOUBT ☐ 64 Ealing ☐ 65 Will Rogers ☐ 66 JUDGE PRIEST ☐ 67 BOOMERANG ☐ 68 RETURN TO GLENNASCAUL ☐ 69 TROUBLE IN PARADISE ☐ 70 DAMES ☐ 71 Norman MacLaren ☐ 72 ON THE TOWN ☐ 73 Frank Capra ☐ 74 It was the first Cinema-scope cartoon ☐ 75 Richard Tauber ☐ 76 Charles Laughton ☐ 77 Robert Flaherty ☐ 78 Charles Bickford ☐ 79 Raymond Massey ☐ 80 Leslie Banks ☐ 81 ALF'S BUTTON AFLOAT ☐ 82 Arthur Knight ☐ 83 Jean Vigo ☐ 84 Walter Wanger ☐ 85 "He couldn't speak words, he went boing-boing instead." ☐ 86 Cartooning ☐ 87 G. W. Pabst ☐ 88 Will Hay ☐ 89 French director Marcel Carné ☐ 90 Lumiere ☐ 91 Harold Lloyd ☐ 92 Paramount ☐ 93 Clark Gable ☐ 94 Laurel and Hardy ☐ 95 STAR SPANGLED RHYTHM ☐ 96 Para-mount ☐ 97 BACK STREET ☐ 98 RED DUST ☐ 99 Trick films ☐ 100 Erich Wolfgang Korngold ☐ 101 Paul Muni ☐ 102 Agnes Ayres ☐ 103 Victor Mature ☐ 104 Thomas Mitchell ☐ 105 BATMAN ☐ 106 Wrong: THE DAIN CURSE remains unfilmed ☐ 107 Lee Majors ☐ Steve Austin ☐ 108 TRIUMPH OF THE WILL ☐ Leni Riefenstahl ☐ 109 George Stevens ☐ 110 Victor Sjostrom ☐ 111 THE PALM BEACH STORY ☐ 112 Gloria Swanson ☐ 113 Tim Holt, playing young George ☐ 114 DEVOTION ☐ 115 Adolph Zukor ☐ 116 Gregg Toland ☐ 117 Buddy Swan ☐ Sonny Bupp ☐ 118 Anti-semitism ☐ 119 Josef Von Stern-berg ☐ 120 SONS OF THE DESERT (GB: FRATER-NALLY YOURS) ☐ 121 Charlie Chase ☐ 122 It was the first Royal Performance Film ☐ 123 George Arliss ☐ 124 W. C. Fields and Mae West ☐ 125 Elmo Lincoln ☐ 126 George Lazenby ☐ 127 INTERMEZZO ☐ 128 Billy Bitzer ☐ 129 ONE MILLION BC/MAN AND HIS MATE ☐ 130 THE THING FROM ANOTHER

WORLD ☐ 131 MONSIEUR BEAUCAIRE ☐ 132 From
the initials of its founders Spoor and Anderson, S 'n A ☐
133 THE GREAT RACE ☐ 134 Henri-Georges
Clouzot ☐ 135 THE BEST YEARS OF OUR LIVES ☐
a handless ex-serviceman, which he was ☐ 136 Lynn
Belvedere ☐ 137 Betty Grable ☐ Dan Dailey ☐ 138 Sam
Levene ☐ 139 ZIEGFELD GIRL ☐ 140 Charles
Winninger ☐ 141 NATIONAL VELVET ☐ 142
CLAUDIA AND DAVID ☐ 143 MEET ME IN ST
LOUIS ☐ 144 Mary Astor ☐ Leon Ames ☐ 145 Nigel
Bruce ☐ 146 Wilfred Lawson ☐ 147 Lon Chaney Jnr ☐
148 Pepe Le Moko ☐ 149 Billie Burke ☐ 150 Theodore
Roberts ☐ 151 Maria Ouspenskaya ☐ 152 Rupert Julian ☐
153 John Gilbert ☐ 154 King Vidor ☐ 155 Gary
Cooper ☐ 156 Emil Jannings ☐ 157 Alan Crosland ☐
158 William Randolph Hearst ☐ 159 Walt Disney: they
are Silly Symphonies of the thirties ☐ 160 GONE WITH
THE WIND ☐ 161 Warner ☐ 162 Universal ☐ 163
ANCHORS AWEIGH ☐ 164 DANGEROUS WHEN
WET ☐ 165 Gene Tierney ☐ 166 Richard Crenna ☐
Samantha Eggar ☐ 167 UP IN ARMS ☐ 168 THE MAN
WHO CAME TO DINNER ☐ 169 May Robson ☐ 170
POCKETFUL OF MIRACLES ☐ 171 KING
KONG ☐ 172 W. C. Fields ☐ 173 SECRETS ☐ 174
THE MOON'S A BALLOON ☐ 175 BRING ON THE
EMPTY HORSES ☐ 176 FANCY PANTS ☐ 177
BLACKMAIL ☐ 178 THE BLUE ANGEL ☐ 179
Harry Langdon ☐ 180 Jean Renoir ☐ 181 Naunton
Wayne ☐ Basil Radford ☐ 182 SPELLBOUND ☐
183 Mary Pickford ☐ D. W. Griffith ☐ 184 Max
Fleischer ☐ 185 Anna Neagle ☐ 186 Rene Clair ☐
187 Luis Bunuel ☐ 188 Rondo Hatton ☐ 189 Ludwig
Donath ☐ 190 NINOTCHKA ☐ 191 THE MIRACLE
OF MORGAN'S CREEK ☐ 192 I MARRIED A
WITCH ☐ 193 THE BEAST FROM 20,000 FATH-
OMS ☐ 194 Charles Lang Jnr ☐ 195 THE CURE ☐
196 Charles Winninger ☐ 197 Joe E. Brown ☐ 198 THE

GREEN PASTURES ☐ 199 Rex Ingram ☐ 200 Mischa Auer ☐ 201 Rosalind Russell ☐ 202 ESCAPE IN THE DESERT ☐ 203 George Cukor ☐ 204 Evelyn Keyes ☐ 205 Boxing and its attendant corruptions ☐ 206 John Barrymore ☐ 207 Alice Brady ☐ IN OLD CHICAGO ☐ 208 WINGS ☐ 209 WATCH ON THE RHINE ☐ 210 LIVING IT UP ☐ Jerry Lewis ☐ 211 The old lady in NIGHT MUST FALL ☐ 212 Tommy Kelly ☐ 213 Fritz Lang ☐ 214 Robert Wiene ☐ 215 Robert Cummings ☐ 216 Tallulah Bankhead ☐ 217 Cecil B. De Mille ☐ 218 A prologue showing American airmen over Rome ☐ 219 STEAMBOAT WILLIE ☐ 220 James Whale ☐ 221 MOROCCO ☐ 222 Eileen Herlie ☐ 223 THE BARKLEYS OF BROADWAY ☐ 224 Henry Daniell ☐ 225 a leopard ☐ 226 Kay Kendall – or the clever ones may say Eddie Calvert on the sound track ☐ 227 Leo McCarey ☐ 228 Walter Huston ☐ 229 Ernest Thesiger ☐ 230 Mischa Auer ☐ 231 Lilli Palmer ☐ 232 Theodore Roosevelt ☐ Sidney Blackmer ☐ 233 A dog owned by Laurel and Hardy ☐ 234 GREEN FOR DANGER ☐ Alastair Sim ☐ 235 General Sternwood ☐ 236 Finlay Currie ☐ 237 Eddie Cantor ☐ 238 Gertrude Lawrence ☐ Elsa Lanchester ☐ 239 Thumper ☐ 240 Felix Salten ☐ 241 Ponchielli's DANCE OF THE HOURS ☐ 242 Lewis Milestone ☐ 243 The Nicholas Brothers ☐ 244 Al ☐ Jim ☐ Harry ☐ 245 Patty ☐ Maxine ☐ La Verne ☐ 246 THE CARPETBAGGERS ☐ 247 Ralph Richardson ☐ 248 Ryan O'Neal ☐ 249 Ralph Richardson ☐ 250 Barbara O'Neil ☐ 251 TO BE OR NOT TO BE ☐ 252 Dana Wynter ☐ Kevin McCarthy ☐

Your score out of a possible 275 :

THE OLD SCHOOLHOUSE DOOR

1 GOODBYE MR CHIPS ☐ 2 VICE VERSA ☐ 3 THE FAILING OF RAYMOND ☐ 4 THE BLACKBOARD JUNGLE ☐ 5 TERM OF TRIAL ☐ 6 THE HAPPIEST

DAYS OF YOUR LIFE ☐ 7 GOOD MORNING MISS DOVE ☐ 8 THE HOUSEMASTER ☐ 9 THE BLUE ANGEL ☐ 10 GOODBYE MR CHIPS (musical version) ☐ 11 THE CORN IS GREEN ☐ 12 TO SIR WITH LOVE ☐ 13 UNMAN WITTERING AND ZIGO ☐ 14 THE PRIME OF MISS JEAN BRODIE ☐ 15 TWO LOVES/SPINSTER ☐ 16 UP THE DOWN STAIRCASE ☐
Your score out of a possible 16:

Answer to POSTER 1: A MAN COULD GET KILLED
☐

WORLD WAR TWO

1 JOURNEY FOR MARGARET ☐ 2 Nobody. The script had it that "in the Army Air Force, any fellow who is a right fellow is called Joe" ☐ 3 NORTH STAR ☐ 4 THE WHITE CLIFFS OF DOVER ☐ 5 Alice Duer Miller ☐ 6 Katharine Hepburn ☐ 7 Errol Flynn ☐ 8 DESTINA-TION TOKYO ☐ 9 MRS MINIVER ☐ 10 Betty Grable ☐ 11 Conrad Veidt ☐ NAZI AGENT ☐ 12 AIR FORCE ☐ 13 HITLER'S CHILDREN ☐ 14 Walter Huston ☐ 15 SO PROUDLY WE HAIL ☐ 16 CRY HAVOC ☐ 17 Kay Francis ☐ 18 Spencer Tracy ☐ 19 OBJECTIVE BURMA ☐ 20 THE PRIDE OF THE MARINES ☐
Your score out of a possible 21:

BILLY THE KID

1 Jack Buetel ☐ 2 Michael J. Pollard ☐ 3 Paul Newman ☐ 4 Johnny Mack Brown ☐ 5 Robert Taylor ☐ 6 Chuck Courtney ☐ 7 Anthony Dexter ☐ 8 Scott Brady ☐ 9 Roy Rogers ☐ 10 Geoffrey Deuel ☐
Your score out of a possible 10:

Answer to POSTER 2: EYE OF THE CAT ☐

LADDERGRAM 1

WALLY CAMPBELL is BOB HOPE ☐ in THE CAT AND THE CANARY ☐
servant WILLIE BEST ☐ THE GHOST BREAKERS ☐
frightened heroine PAULETTE GODDARD ☐ THE CAT AND THE CANARY or THE GHOST BREAKERS ☐
flyer KATHERINE HEPBURN ☐ THE IRON PETTI-COAT ☐
health farm director BETTY HUTTON ☐ LET'S FACE IT ☐
servant GALE SONDERGAARD ☐ THE CAT AND THE CANARY ☐
Nazi spy OTTO PREMINGER ☐ THEY GOT ME COVERED ☐
vaudevillian JAMES CAGNEY ☐ THE SEVEN LITTLE FOYS ☐
Your score out of a possible 16:

THE WARNERS DO IT AGAIN

1 THE MALE ANIMAL ☐ 2 ONE SUNDAY AFTER-NOON ☐ 3 OIL FOR THE LAMPS OF CHINA ☐
4 THE MOUTHPIECE ☐ 5 THE SEA WOLF ☐
6 THE MAN WHO PLAYED GOD ☐ 7 THE GOLD-DIGGERS and GOLDDIGGERS OF 1933 ☐ 8 THE LIFE OF JIMMY DOLAN ☐ 9 ONE WAY PASS-AGE ☐ 10 FOUR DAUGHTERS ☐ 11 OUTWARD BOUND ☐ 12 CAGED ☐ 13 KID GALAHAD ☐
14 TWENTY THOUSAND YEARS IN SING SING ☐
15 THE MILLIONAIRE ☐ 16 THE MALTESE FAL-CON ☐ 17 A SLIGHT CASE OF MURDER ☐
18 THREE FACES EAST ☐ 19 HIGH SIERRA ☐
20 THE PETRIFIED FOREST ☐ 21 TO HAVE AND HAVE NOT ☐ 22 THE LETTER ☐ 23 THE CROWD

ROARS ☐   24 DANGEROUS ☐   25 FIVE STAR
FINAL ☐
Your score out of a possible 25:

THE TELEHEROES

1 Ty Hardin ☐ 2 Mike Connors ☐ 3 James Garner ☐ Jack
Kelly ☐ Roger Moore ☐ 4 William Conrad ☐ 5 Judd
Hirsch ☐ 6 George Nader ☐ 7 Edward Woodward ☐
8 David Birney ☐ 9 Burt Reynolds ☐ 10 Raymond Burr ☐
11 Dennis Weaver ☐ 12 George Peppard ☐ 13 Howard
Duff ☐ 14 John Cassavetes ☐ 15 Ray Milland ☐ 16 David
Janssen ☐ 17 Richard Denning ☐ 18 Phil Carey ☐ 19 Skip
Homeier ☐ 20 Gene Barry ☐ 21 Craig Stevens ☐ 22 Dan
Duryea ☐ 23 Jack Lord ☐ 24 Lloyd Bridges ☐
Your score out of a possible 26:

Answer to POSTER 3: TAKE MY LIFE ☐

LADDERGRAM 2

CRYSTAL ALLEN is JOAN CRAWFORD ☐ in THE
   WOMEN ☐
flyer JOHN WAYNE ☐ REUNION IN FRANCE ☐
ex-husband ROSSANO BRAZZI ☐ THE STORY OF
   ESTHER COSTELLO/THE GOLDEN VIRGIN ☐
killer JACK PALANCE ☐ SUDDEN FEAR ☐
plastic surgeon MELVYN DOUGLAS ☐ A WOMAN'S
   FACE ☐
western lady MERCEDES McCAMBRIDGE ☐ JOHNNY
   GUITAR ☐
violinist JOHN GARFIELD ☐ HUMORESQUE ☐
walker HARRY LANGDON ☐ TRAMP TRAMP
   TRAMP ☐
ice skater JAMES STEWART ☐ ICE FOLLIES OF
   1939 ☐

lover victim VAN HEFLIN ☐ POSSESSED ☐
poetic postman FRANCHOT TONE ☐ THE BRIDE
   WORE RED ☐
friend EVE ARDEN ☐ MILDRED PIERCE ☐
blind pianist MICHAEL WILDING ☐ TORCH SONG ☐
Your score out of a possible 26 :

IN TWO WORDS, IM POSSIBLE

1 IT GROWS ON TREES ☐ 2 ONCE UPON A TIME ☐
3 IT'S A WONDERFUL LIFE ☐   4 TOPPER RE-
TURNS ☐   5 BOBBIKINS ☐   6 BIRDS DO IT ☐
7 SHADOW OF THE CAT ☐   8 THE NEXT VOICE
YOU HEAR ☐   9 THE ABSENT-MINDED PROFES-
SOR ☐   10 IT HAPPENS EVERY SPRING ☐   11 YOU
NEVER CAN TELL (GB: YOU NEVER KNOW) ☐
12 FANTASTIC VOYAGE ☐   13 WHAT'S SO BAD
ABOUT FEELING GOOD? ☐   14 THE INCREDIBLE
MR LIMPET ☐   15 THE INCREDIBLE SHRINKING
MAN ☐ 16 RHUBARB ☐
Your score out of a possible 16 :

LADDERGRAM 3

KAREL CERNIK is FREDRIC MARCH ☐ in MAN ON
   A TIGHTROPE ☐
frivolous lady JOAN CRAWFORD ☐ in SUSAN AND
   GOD/THE GAY MRS TREXEL ☐
defence counsel SPENCER TRACY ☐ INHERIT THE
   WIND ☐
warlock CECIL KELLAWAY ☐ I MARRIED A
   WITCH ☐
wife MILDRED DUNNOCK ☐ DEATH OF A SALES-
   MAN ☐
escaped convict HUMPHREY BOGART ☐ THE
   DESPERATE HOURS ☐

writer's wife ALEXIS SMITH ☐ THE ADVENTURES
  OF MARK TWAIN ☐
queen FLORENCE ELDRIDGE ☐ CHRISTOPHER
  COLUMBUS ☐
shady lady MIRIAM HOPKINS ☐ DR JEKYLL AND
  MR HYDE ☐
playwright's wife LORETTA YOUNG ☐ BEDTIME
  STORY ☐
employee GREGORY PECK ☐ THE MAN IN THE
  GREY FLANNEL SUIT ☐
general BURT LANCASTER ☐ SEVEN DAYS IN
  MAY ☐
pursuing policeman CHARLES LAUGHTON ☐ LES
  MISERABLES ☐
Your score out of a possible 26:

ALFRED HITCHCOCK PRESENTS

1 THE WRONG MAN ☐　　2 STRANGERS ON A
TRAIN ☐　　3 YOUNG AND INNOCENT (US: THE
GIRL WAS YOUNG) ☐　4 THE 39 STEPS ☐　5 THE
PLEASURE GARDEN ☐　　6 THE LODGER ☐　　7
MURDER ☐ 8 PSYCHO ☐ 9 ROPE ☐ LIFEBOAT ☐
10 FOREIGN CORRESPONDENT ☐　11 THE SECRET
AGENT ☐　　　12 SABOTAGE (US: A WOMAN
ALONE) ☐ 13 THE MANXMAN ☐ 14 SABOTEUR ☐
15 BLACKMAIL ☐　16 THE MAN WHO KNEW TOO
MUCH (1934) ☐　　17 NORTH BY NORTHWEST ☐
18 LIFEBOAT ☐　19 SPELLBOUND ☐　20 UNDER
CAPRICORN ☐
Your score out of a possible 21:

Answer to POSTER 4: THE THIRD SECRET ☐

OSCAR, I LOVE YOU

1 ANTHONY ADVERSE ☐ 2 STAGECOACH ☐ 3 GOING MY WAY ☐ 4 DANGEROUS ☐ JEZEBEL ☐ 5 A DOUBLE LIFE ☐ 6 COME AND GET IT ☐ IN OLD KENTUCKY ☐ THE WESTERNER ☐ 7 THE SIN OF MADELON CLAUDET ☐ AIRPORT ☐ 8 MIN AND BILL ☐ 9 WATCH ON THE RHINE ☐ 10 KITTY FOYLE ☐ 11 SUSPICION ☐ 12 YANKEE DOODLE DANDY ☐ 13 MORNING GLORY ☐ GUESS WHO'S COMING TO DINNER ☐ THE LION IN WINTER ☐ 14 THE DIVINE LADY ☐ CAVALCADE ☐ 15 THE AWFUL TRUTH ☐ GOING MY WAY ☐ He also received one for writing LOVE AFFAIR ☐ 16 SKIPPY ☐ 17 CASABLANCA ☐

Your score out of a possible 26:

SILENCE PLEASE I

1 MOBY DICK ☐ 2 Jackie Coogan ☐ 3 THE JAZZ SINGER ☐ 4 INTOLERANCE ☐ 5 Lon Chaney ☐ 6 Gloria Swanson ☐ 7 Belle Bennett ☐ 8 Richard Barthelmess ☐ 9 Guy Newall ☐ 10 George Robey ☐ 11 Ethel Barrymore ☐ 12 Bert Lytell ☐ 13 Rudolph Valentino ☐ 14 SAFETY LAST ☐ 15 GREED ☐ 16 Erich Von Stroheim ☐ 17 Laurel and Hardy ☐ 18 HE WHO GETS SLAPPED ☐ 19 THE SQUAW MAN ☐ 20 Conrad Veidt ☐

Your score out of a possible 20:

COPYCATS: FIRST DIVISION

1 They all played angels ☐ : THE BISHOP'S WIFE ☐ HEAVEN ONLY KNOWS ☐ HERE COMES MR JORDAN ☐

2 They all dressed as women ☐ : I WAS A MALE WAR

BRIDE ☐ SOME LIKE IT HOT ☐ YOU'RE IN THE
ARMY NOW ☐

3 They all played Shakespearean actors ☐ : A DOUBLE
LIFE ☐ TO BE OR NOT TO BE ☐ PRINCE OF
PLAYERS ☐

4 They all played The Scarlet Pimpernel ☐ : RETURN
OF THE SCARLET PIMPERNEL ☐ THE SCAR-
LET PIMPERNEL ☐ THE ELUSIVE PIMPER-
NEL ☐

5 They all impersonated great entertainers ☐ : THE
EDDIE CANTOR STORY ☐ THE JOLSON STORY
☐ FUNNY GIRL/FUNNY LADY ☐

6 They all played DR JEKYLL AND MR HYDE ☐

7 They all played Queen Victoria ☐ : THE MUD-
LARK ☐ VICTORIA THE GREAT or SIXTY
GLORIOUS YEARS ☐ THE PRIME MINISTER ☐

8 They all played famous composers ☐ : Sousa in STARS
AND STRIPES FOREVER (GB: MARCHING
ALONG) ☐ Tchaikovsky in THE MUSIC LOVERS ☐
Sullivan in THE STORY OF GILBERT AND SULLI-
VAN ☐ Handel in THE GREAT MR HANDEL ☐

9 They all performed (or appeared to) on the flying trap-
eze ☐ : THE THREE MAXIMS ☐ TRAPEZE ☐
THE GREATEST SHOW ON EARTH ☐ AT THE
CIRCUS ☐

10 They all played Disraeli ☐ : THE PRIME MINISTER
☐ DISRAELI ☐ THE MUDLARK ☐

11 They all played leprechauns ☐ : THE LUCK OF THE
IRISH ☐ DARBY O'GILL AND THE LITTLE
PEOPLE ☐ FINIAN'S RAINBOW ☐ JACK THE
GIANT KILLER ☐

12 They all played visitors from outer space ☐ : THE DAY
THE EARTH STOOD STILL ☐ THIS ISLAND
EARTH ☐ THE THING FROM ANOTHER WORLD
☐ NOT OF THIS EARTH ☐

13 They all played the invisible man ☐ : ABBOTT AND
COSTELLO MEET THE INVISIBLE MAN ☐

INVISIBLE AGENT or THE INVISIBLE MAN'S REVENGE ☐ THE INVISIBLE MAN RETURNS ☐

14 They all had split personalities ☐ : MADONNA OF THE SEVEN MOONS ☐ THE THREE FACES OF EVE ☐ LIZZIE ☐

15 They all played US Presidents ☐ : FAIL SAFE (and others) ☐ ADVISE AND CONSENT ☐ SEVEN DAYS IN MAY ☐ DR STRANGELOVE ☐

16 They all served time on Devil's Island ☐ : PASSAGE TO MARSEILLES ☐ CONDEMNED ☐ PAPILLON ☐ THE LIFE OF EMILE ZOLA ☐

17 They all played giants ☐ : ATTACK OF THE FIFTY FOOT WOMAN ☐ JACK AND THE BEANSTALK ☐ THE AMAZING COLOSSAL MAN ☐

18 They all played the Devil ☐ : ALIAS NICK BEAL ☐ ALL THAT MONEY CAN BUY ☐ HEAVEN CAN WAIT ☐

19 They all made journeys by air balloon ☐ : THE WIZARD OF OZ ☐ CHARLIE BUBBLES ☐ AROUND THE WORLD IN EIGHTY DAYS ☐

20 They all played Death ☐ : ON BORROWED TIME ☐ ORPHEE ☐ DEATH TAKES A HOLIDAY ☐

21 They all played famous pirates ☐ : THE BUCCANEER ☐ ANNE OF THE INDIES ☐ BLACKBEARD THE PIRATE ☐

22 They all played Calamity Jane ☐ : CALAMITY JANE AND SAM BASS ☐ CALAMITY JANE ☐ THE PLAINSMAN ☐

23 They all played ventriloquists ☐ : THE GREAT GABBO ☐ KNOCK ON WOOD ☐ DEAD OF NIGHT ☐

24 They all played Henry VIII ☐ : THE PRINCE AND THE PAUPER ☐ THE PRIVATE LIFE OF HENRY VIII ☐ CARRY ON HENRY ☐

25 They all played the Bronte sisters ☐ in DEVOTION ☐

26 They all played Wyatt Earp ☐ : HOUR OF THE

GUN ☐ GUNFIGHT AT THE OK CORRAL ☐ MY
DARLING CLEMENTINE ☐

27 They all played Hitler ☐ : Watson innumerable times
   but principally in THE HITLER GANG ☐ THE
   MAGIC FACE ☐ HITLER ☐

28 They all played oriental detectives who had series to
   themselves ☐ : Mr Wong ☐ Charlie Chan ☐ Mr
   Moto ☐

29 They all played ghosts ☐ : BLITHE SPIRIT ☐ THE
   GHOST GOES WEST ☐ THE GHOST AND MRS
   MUIR ☐

30 They all played alcoholics ☐ : DAYS OF WINE AND
   ROSES ☐ COME FILL THE CUP ☐ THE LOST
   WEEKEND ☐

Your score out of a possible 121 :

LADDERGRAM 4

KERRY BRADFORD is ERROL FLYNN ☐ in
   VIRGINIA CITY ☐
patriot ANN SHERIDAN ☐ EDGE OF DARKNESS ☐
usurper CLAUDE RAINS ☐ THE ADVENTURES OF
   ROBIN HOOD ☐
pirate BASIL RATHBONE ☐ CAPTAIN BLOOD ☐
queen FLORA ROBSON ☐ THE SEA HAWK ☐
actress DOROTHY MALONE ☐ TOO MUCH TOO
   SOON ☐
C O's wife KAY FRANCIS ☐ ANOTHER DAWN ☐
Henry VIII MONTAGU LOVE ☐ THE PRINCE AND
   THE PAUPER ☐
villain HENRY DANIELL ☐ THE SEA HAWK ☐
Nazi RAYMOND MASSEY ☐ DESPERATE
   JOURNEY ☐
dancer ANNA NEAGLE ☐ LILACS IN THE SPRING
   ☐ (US : LET'S MAKE UP)
Your score out of a possible 22 :

Answer to POSTER 5 : THE LAST WAGON ☐

IT STARTED THIS WAY

1 REBECCA ☐   2 LOST HORIZON ☐   3 CITIZEN
KANE ☐ 4 JOURNEY INTO FEAR ☐ 5 THE GRAPES
OF WRATH ☐   6 LITTLE CAESAR ☐   7 BEAU
GESTE ☐   8 ON THE TOWN ☐   9 DESTRY RIDES
AGAIN ☐   10 TROUBLE IN PARADISE ☐   11 THE
PHILADELPHIA STORY ☐   12 THE BIG SLEEP ☐
13 BAD DAY AT BLACK ROCK ☐   14 ALL ABOUT
EVE ☐   15 DOUBLE INDEMNITY ☐   16 SINGIN' IN
THE RAIN ☐   17 THE THIRD MAN ☐   18 NINO-
TCHKA ☐   19 A NIGHT AT THE OPERA ☐   20
HEAVEN CAN WAIT ☐ 21 I'M ALL RIGHT JACK ☐
22 INVASION OF THE BODY SNATCHERS ☐ 23 THE
INVISIBLE MAN ☐   24 IN WHICH WE SERVE ☐
25 KING KONG (1933) ☐
Your score out of a possible 25 :

TUT, TUT

1 Joan Crawford ☐   2 THE MOON IS BLUE ☐   3
"Frankly, my dear, I don't give a damn" ☐ 4 Ben Hecht ☐
5 SANCTUARY ☐ William Faulkner ☐ 6 Mae West ☐
SHE DONE HIM WRONG ☐ 7 Edward Albee ☐ 8 The
scene in which the bachelors watch blue movies ☐   9 Beryl
Reid ☐ Susannah York ☐ Coral Browne ☐ 10 EXTASE
or ECSTASY ☐ Gustav Machaty ☐   11 "Move your
bloomin' arse" ☐   12 THE WICKED LADY ☐   13 Alec
Guinness' Fagin was held to be anti-Semitic ☐ 14 DON'T
GO NEAR THE WATER ☐ 15 A FLEA IN HER EAR ☐
Your score out of a possible 20 :

FLASHBACK

1 SUNSET BOULEVARD ☐ 2 DEAD RECKONING ☐
3 THE GREAT McGINTY ☐   4 HOLD BACK THE

DAWN ☐   5 THE BRIDE OF FRANKENSTEIN ☐
6 REBECCA ☐ 7 THE MOON AND SIXPENCE or THE
RAZOR'S EDGE ☐ (In both of which he played Somerset
Maugham) 8 ENCHANTMENT ☐ 9 THE LAVENDER
HILL MOB ☐   10 ROXIE HART ☐   11 ROAD TO
UTOPIA ☐ 12 EDWARD MY SON ☐   13 THE TEA-
HOUSE OF THE AUGUST MOON ☐   14 KIND
HEARTS AND CORONETS ☐   15 WUTHERING
HEIGHTS ☐
Your score out of a possible 15 :

LADDERGRAM 5

GRAY is BORIS KARLOFF ☐ in THE BODY
   SNATCHER ☐
second lead JOHN BOLES ☐ FRANKENSTEIN ☐
hunchback J. CARROL NAISH ☐ HOUSE OF FRANK-
   ENSTEIN ☐
rich man GEORGE ARLISS ☐ THE HOUSE OF
   ROTHSCHILD ☐
investigator LEWIS STONE ☐ THE MASK OF FU
   MANCHU ☐
chess player BELA LUGOSI ☐ THE BLACK CAT ☐
nervous hero DANNY KAYE ☐ THE SECRET LIFE OF
   WALTER MITTY ☐
scientist BASIL RATHBONE ☐ SON OF FRANKEN-
   STEIN ☐
bird-man PETER LORRE ☐ THE RAVEN ☐
gangster PAUL MUNI ☐ SCARFACE ☐
stranded guest MELVYN DOUGLAS ☐ THE OLD
   DARK HOUSE ☐
opera singer SUSANNA FOSTER ☐ THE CLIMAX ☐
newspaper publisher VAN HEFLIN ☐ TAP ROOTS ☐
Your score out of a possible 26 :

Answer to POSTER 6: THREE INTO TWO WON'T GO
   ☐

THEY WENT TO THE MOVIES

1 CAPRICE ☐   2 JOLSON SINGS AGAIN ☐   3 THE
SPIRAL STAIRCASE ☐   4 THE HAPPY TIME ☐
5 CONQUEST OF SPACE ☐   6 BRUTE FORCE ☐
7 ENSIGN PULVER ☐ 8 SULLIVAN'S TRAVELS ☐
9 EACH DAWN I DIE ☐   10 THE LAST PICTURE
SHOW ☐   11 THE SMALLEST SHOW ON EARTH
(US: BIG TIME OPERATORS) ☐   12 SUNSET
BOULEVARD ☐
Your score out of a possible 12:

THEY SUFFERED A SEA CHANGE I

1 A BIG HAND FOR THE LITTLE LADY ☐   2
HARPER ☐   3 NEVER GIVE A SUCKER AN EVEN
BREAK ☐ 4 INTERMEZZO ☐ 5 GASLIGHT ☐ (The
British had their own excellent version of GASLIGHT,
which was virtually suppressed in the US.)   6 THE FLIM
FLAM MAN ☐ 7 AMERICA, AMERICA ☐ 8 BROAD-
WAY BILL ☐   9 HOLIDAY ☐ (Also called FREE TO
LIVE) 10 ANY WEDNESDAY ☐ 11 THE BATCHELOR
AND THE BOBBYSOXER ☐ 12 THE ENFORCER ☐
13 THE COURT MARTIAL OF BILLY MITCHELL ☐
14 CIRCUS WORLD ☐ 15 EXPERIMENT IN TERROR
☐ 16 THE NEW CENTURIONS ☐ 17 FOOL'S PAR-
ADE ☐   18 STATE OF THE UNION ☐   19 OUT OF
THE PAST ☐   20 ONE MILLION BC ☐
Your score out of a possible 20:

UP TO DATE

1 Paramount ☐   2 Peter Bogdanovich ☐   3 Stanley
Donen ☐ 4 Billy Rose ☐ 5 Peter Benchley ☐ 6 Tony
Curtis ☐ 7 THE MAIDS ☐ 8 Ants ☐ 9 Saul Bass ☐
Designing credit sequences ☐ 10 Anne Bancroft ☐ 11 Blake
Edwards ☐·12 Robert Towne ☐ 13 Theodore Roosevelt ☐

14 Puppet films ☐ George Pal ☐   15 Charlotte Rampling ☐   16 Marseilles ☐   17 Buford Pusser ☐   18 Vancouver ☐ 19 Max Von Sydow ☐ 20 SIX DAYS OF THE CONDOR ☐   21 W W AND THE DIXIE DANCE-KINGS ☐   22 Douglas Wilmer ☐ Thorley Walters ☐
23 John Alcott ☐   24 Lee Patrick ☐ Elisha Cook Jnr ☐
25 THE DROWNING POOL ☐
Your score out of a possible 29:

Answer to POSTER 7: RAW WIND IN EDEN ☐

LADDERGRAM 6

LINDA SETON is KATHARINE HEPBURN ☐ in HOLIDAY ☐

son DEAN STOCKWELL ☐ LONG DAY'S JOURNEY INTO NIGHT ☐

holiday acquaintance ROSSANO BRAZZI ☐ SUMMER-TIME/SUMMER HOLIDAY ☐

husband PETER O'TOOLE ☐ THE LION IN WINTER ☐

soldier FRANCHOT TONE ☐ QUALITY STREET ☐

cowboy JOHN WAYNE ☐ ROOSTER COGBURN ☐

ex-husband CARY GRANT ☐ THE PHILADELPHIA STORY ☐

future son-in-law SIDNEY POITIER ☐ GUESS WHO'S COMING TO DINNER ☐

composer PAUL HENREID ☐ SONG OF LOVE ☐

producer ADOLPHE MENJOU ☐ MORNING GLORY or STAGE DOOR ☐

father WALTER HUSTON ☐ DRAGON SEED ☐

reporter SPENCER TRACY ☐ KEEPER OF THE FLAME ☐

skipper HUMPHREY BOGART ☐ THE AFRICAN QUEEN ☐

flyer BOB HOPE ☐ THE IRON PETTICOAT ☐

teacher PAUL LUKAS ☐ LITTLE WOMEN ☐
industrialist husband ROBERT TAYLOR ☐ UNDER-
   CURRENT ☐
politician COLIN CLIVE ☐ CHRISTOPHER
   STRONG ☐
Your score out of a possible 34 :

REMAKE ROLES

1 Mrs Wiggs ☐ MRS WIGGS OF THE CABBAGE
PATCH (1934 and 1942) ☐   2 The sinister husband ☐
LOVE FROM A STRANGER (1937 and 1946) ☐   3 The
grandmother ☐ LOVE AFFAIR ☐ AN AFFAIR TO
REMEMBER ☐   4 The frightened heroine ☐ THE
MYSTERY OF THE WAX MUSEUM ☐ HOUSE OF
WAX ☐   5 The heroine ☐ BACHELOR MOTHER ☐
BUNDLE OF JOY ☐   6 The father ☐ A BILL OF
DIVORCEMENT (1932 and 1940) ☐   7 Title role ☐
KIND LADY (1935 and 1951) ☐   8 The hero ☐
BERKELEY SQUARE ☐ I'LL NEVER FORGET YOU
(GB: THE HOUSE IN THE SQUARE) ☐   9 Sir Percy
Blakeney ☐   THE SCARLET PIMPERNEL ☐   THE
ELUSIVE PIMPERNEL ☐   10 The dying heroine ☐
DARK VICTORY ☐ STOLEN HOURS ☐ 11 The heart-
less heroine ☐   THE DEVIL IS A WOMAN (1935 and
1950) ☐   12 Title role ☐ MONSIEUR BEAUCAIRE
(1924 and 1946) ☐   13 Hildy Johnson ☐ THE FRONT
PAGE ☐ HIS GIRL FRIDAY ☐ 14 The supposedly ailing
heroine/hero ☐ NOTHING SACRED ☐ LIVING IT
UP ☐ 15 The adult travelling half fare ☐ THE MAJOR
AND THE MINOR ☐ YOU'RE NEVER TOO
YOUNG ☐   16 The butler ☐ RUGGLES OF RED
GAP ☐ FANCY PANTS ☐ 17 Charley ☐ CHARLEY'S
AUNT (1930 and 1941) ☐ 18 Chang ☐ LOST HORIZON
(1937 and 1973) ☐   19 The publicity man ☐ A STAR IS
BORN (1937 and 1954) ☐ 20 The doctor ☐ DR SOCRA-
TES ☐ KING OF THE UNDERWORLD ☐   21 The

newspaper reporter ☐ IT HAPPENED ONE NIGHT ☐
YOU CAN'T RUN AWAY FROM IT ☐ 22 The frightened
wife ☐ THE MAN WHO KNEW TOO MUCH (1934 and
1956) ☐ 23 Title role ☐ GUNGA DIN ☐ SERGEANTS
THREE (corresponding role) ☐ 24 The Tin Man ☐ THE
WIZARD OF OZ (1924 and 1939) ☐ 25 Dolly ☐ THE
MATCHMAKER ☐ HELLO DOLLY ☐ 26 The mature
boarder ☐ THE MORE THE MERRIER ☐ WALK
DON'T RUN ☐ 27 Eliza ☐ PYGMALION ☐ MY FAIR
LADY ☐ 28 Title role ☐ CLEOPATRA (1918 and
1934) ☐ 29 Mrs Micawber ☐ DAVID COPPERFIELD
(1935 and 1969) ☐ 30 Van Helsing ☐ DRACULA ☐
(several appearances in thirties and fifties/seventies respectively)
Your score out of a possible 76 :

THE VERY MAN

1 Paul Scofield ☐ 2 James Earl Jones ☐ 3 Claude Rains ☐
4 Lon Chaney Jnr ☐ 5 James Mason ☐ 6 Nils Asther ☐
7 James Stewart ☐ 8 Glenn Ford ☐ 9 Ray Milland ☐
10 Jack Benny ☐ 11 Jean Louis Trintignant ☐ 12 Francis
Lederer ☐ 13 Alec Guinness ☐ 14 Gregory Peck ☐
15 James Cagney ☐ 16 George C. Scott ☐ 17 Kirk
Douglas ☐ 18 Cliff Robertson ☐ 19 Lewis Stone ☐
20 Frank Sinatra ☐ 21 Ronald Colman ☐ 22 Monty Woolley ☐ 23 In the original film not William Powell, but
Edward Ellis ☐ 24 Claude Rains ☐ 25 George Arliss ☐
26 Edward Ellis ☐ 27 Anton Diffring ☐ 28 Henry
Fonda ☐ 29 Burt Reynolds ☐ 30 John Wayne (though
Jimmy Stewart thought he did it) ☐
Your score out of a possible 30 :

NO SUB-TITLES REQUIRED

1 THE LONG NIGHT ☐ Henry Fonda ☐ 2 LURED/
PERSONAL COLUMN ☐ George Sanders ☐ 3 THE
OUTRAGE ☐ Paul Newman ☐ 4 HUMAN DESIRE ☐

Glenn Ford ☐   5 MIDNIGHT EPISODE ☐ Stanley
Holloway ☐   6 THE UNFINISHED DANCE ☐ Cyd
Charisse ☐ 7 MAD LOVE ☐ Colin Clive ☐ 8 ALGIERS
☐ Charles Boyer ☐ or CASBAH ☐ Tony Martin ☐
9 STRANGER IN THE HOUSE (US: COP OUT) ☐
James Mason ☐ 10 A FISTFUL OF DOLLARS ☐ Clint
Eastwood ☐ 11 THE THIRTEENTH LETTER ☐ Charles
Boyer ☐   12 THE MAGNIFICENT SEVEN ☐ Yul
Brynner ☐
Your score out of a possible 24:

LADDERGRAM 7

JOE LELAND is FRANK SINATRA ☐ in THE
  DETECTIVE ☐
former U-boat commander ALF KJELLIN ☐ ASSAULT
  ON A QUEEN ☐
older brother EDWARD G. ROBINSON ☐ A HOLE IN
  THE HEAD ☐
Captain Trumbull CARY GRANT ☐ THE PRIDE AND
  THE PASSION ☐
hood DEAN MARTIN ☐ ROBIN AND THE SEVEN
  HOODS ☐
rich girl GRACE KELLY ☐ HIGH SOCIETY ☐
sergeant BURT LANCASTER ☐ FROM HERE TO
  ETERNITY ☐
younger brother TONY BILL ☐ COME BLOW YOUR
  HORN ☐
sergeant DEAN MARTIN ☐ SERGEANTS THREE ☐
nurse OLIVIA DE HAVILLAND ☐ NOT AS A
  STRANGER ☐
south sea priest SPENCER TRACY ☐ THE DEVIL AT
  FOUR O'CLOCK ☐
cripple ELEANOR PARKER ☐ THE MAN WITH THE
  GOLDEN ARM ☐
singer VIVIAN BLAINE ☐ GUYS AND DOLLS ☐
Your score out of a possible 26:

WHAT'S IN A NAME?

1 HELP ☐ 2 ARRIVEDERCI BABY / DROP DEAD DARLING ☐ 3 LOST COMMAND ☐ 4 MONSIEUR VERDOUX ☐ 5 I COULD GO ON SINGING ☐ 6 RANCHO NOTORIOUS ☐ 7 MONKEY BUSINESS (1951) ☐ 8 THE SPIRAL STAIRCASE ☐ 9 THE 'HONEYPOT ☐ 10 A LETTER TO THREE WIVES ☐ 11 SOME LIKE IT HOT ☐ 12 THE PRIVATE LIVES OF ELIZABETH AND ESSEX ☐ 13 THE TROUBLE WITH ANGELS ☐ 14 BEDTIME STORY (1964) ☐ 15 SEVEN BRIDES FOR SEVEN BROTHERS ☐ 16 THREE COINS IN THE FOUNTAIN ☐ 17 THE BAD AND THE BEAUTIFUL (the original title was later used for a different film) ☐ 18 WHAT A WAY TO GO ☐ THE BAND WAGON ☐ DANCING IN THE DARK ☐ 19 SKY WEST AND CROOKED (US: GYPSY GIRL) ☐ 20 THE HAPPENING ☐ 21 DEADLIER THAN THE MALE ☐ 22 ALVAREZ KELLY ☐ 23 THE GYPSY MOTHS ☐ 24 FLAP (GB: THE LAST WARRIOR) ☐ Your score out of a possible 26:

WHEN DISASTER STRUCK

1 Myrna Loy ☐ Lana Turner ☐ THE RAINS OF RAN-CHIPUR ☐ Louis Bromfield ☐ 2 Dorothy Lamour ☐ THE GREATEST SHOW ON EARTH ☐ 3 Jon Hall ☐ the invisible man ☐ 4 INTOLERANCE ☐ D. W. Griffith ☐ 5 AIRPORT ☐ Arthur Hailey ☐ 6 A NIGHT TO REMEMBER ☐ 1912 ☐ 7 A forest fire ☐ Maurice Maeterlinck ☐ Felix Salten ☐ 8 KRAKATOA: EAST OF JAVA ☐ (Krakatoa is west of Java.) 9 Nero ☐ THE STORY OF MANKIND ☐ QUO VADIS ☐ THE SIGN OF THE CROSS ☐ 10 THE POSEIDON ADVEN-TURE ☐ 11 THE SISTERS ☐ Myron Brinig ☐ 12 FATE IS THE HUNTER ☐ Ernest K. Gann ☐ 13 FOREVER AMBER ☐ Kathleen Winsor ☐ 14 Locusts

☐ Pearl Buck ☐ 15 A coal mine cave in ☐ 16 MORNING DEPARTURE (US: OPERATION DISASTER) ☐ 17 A volcano ☐ Max Catto ☐ 18 George Pal ☐ 19 H. G. Wells ☐ War ☐ Plague ☐ 20 A volcanic eruption ☐ Your score out of a possible 40 :

Answer to POSTER 8 : THE RUSSIANS ARE COMING ☐

BIG JOHN

1 THE SHOOTIST ☐ 2 SHE WORE A YELLOW RIBBON ☐ 3 THE FIGHTING KENTUCKIAN ☐ 4 THE QUIET MAN ☐ 5 BLOOD ALLEY ☐ 6 THE CONQUEROR ☐ 7 JET PILOT ☐ 8 TYCOON ☐ 9 REAP THE WILD WIND ☐ 10 THE GREATEST STORY EVER TOLD ☐ 11 THE SONS OF KATIE ELDER ☐ 12 HATARI ☐ 13 THE BIG TRAIL (1930) ☐ 14 WITHOUT RESERVATIONS ☐ 15 BIG JIM McLAIN ☐ 16 ISLAND IN THE SKY ☐ Your score out of a possible 16 :

FROM THE ORIGINAL PLAY

1 HEAVEN CAN WAIT ☐ 2 HERE COMES MR JORDAN ☐ 3 MIDNIGHT LACE ☐ 4 THE ACTRESS ☐ 5 THE HEIRESS ☐ 6 THE MATCHMAKER or HELLO DOLLY ☐ 7 SHE DONE HIM WRONG ☐ 8 CASABLANCA ☐ 9 LILIOM or CAROUSEL ☐ 10 TWENTIETH CENTURY ☐ 11 SUMMERTIME/ SUMMER MADNESS ☐ 12 BOOM ☐ 13 MOROCCO ☐ 14 THE MAN WHO PLAYED GOD/SINCERELY YOURS ☐ 15 FORBIDDEN PLANET ☐ 16 THE PRINCE AND THE SHOWGIRL ☐ 17 PEOPLE WILL TALK ☐ 18 THIS LOVE OF OURS/ NEVER SAY GOODBYE ☐ 19 CHIMES AT MIDNIGHT/FALSTAFF ☐ 20 ATTACK! ☐ 21 WE'RE NO ANGELS ☐

22 THE STRIPPER (GB: WOMAN OF SUMMER) □
23 OKLAHOMA! □ 24 JOAN OF ARC □
Your score out of a possible 24:

DUCHESS OF HOLLYWOOD

1 ANOTHER MAN'S POISON □   2 IN THIS OUR
LIFE □ 3 THE VIRGIN QUEEN □ 4 JEZEBEL □
5 FRONT PAGE WOMAN □ 6 BORDERTOWN □
7 FOG OVER FRISCO □ DEAD RINGER □ 8 PHONE
CALL FROM A STRANGER □   9 JUNE BRIDE □
10 A STOLEN LIFE □ DEAD RINGER □   11 MR
SKEFFINGTON □ 12 DECEPTION □   13 OLD
ACQUAINTANCE □ 14 THE LETTER □ 15 THE
LITTLE FOXES □ 16 JUAREZ □
Your score out of a possible 18:

A GOOD CAST IS WORTH REPEATING

1 GORILLA AT LARGE □   2 BAD DAY AT BLACK
ROCK □ 3 TWELVE ANGRY MEN □ 4 HOUSE OF
DRACULA □   5 THE OLD DARK HOUSE (1932) □
6 GONE WITH THE WIND □   7 REBECCA □
8 CITIZEN KANE □ 9 THE CAT AND THE CANARY
□ 10 ARSENIC AND OLD LACE □ 11 THE WIZARD
OF OZ □ 12 NINOTCHKA □ 13 TAKE ME OUT TO
THE BALL GAME □   14 YOU'LL FIND OUT □
15 KING KONG □ 16 CAST A GIANT SHADOW □
17 THE GODFATHER □   18 A MAN FOR ALL SEA-
SONS □ 19 AIRPORT □ 20 THE PHILADELPHIA
STORY □ 21 THE QUIET MAN □ 22 THE LADY
VANISHES □ 23 ANATOMY OF A MURDER 24 SEVEN
DAYS IN MAY □ 25 GIANT □ 26 ALL ABOUT EVE □
27 PSYCHO □   28 THE BEST YEARS OF OUR
LIVES □   29 HELLZAPOPPIN □   30 JUAREZ □
31 MR SMITH GOES TO WASHINGTON □ 32 THE
RAINS CAME □ 33 THE WOLF MAN □ 34 KINGS

ROW ☐ 35 LOST HORIZON (1937) ☐ 36 THE AD-
VENTURES OF ROBIN HOOD ☐ 37 THE SEA
HAWK ☐ 38 THE INVISIBLE MAN RETURNS ☐
39 TOWER OF LONDON ☐ 40 TOWER OF LONDON
(1939) ☐ 41 THE RAVEN (1963) ☐ 42 WILSON ☐
43 HEAVEN CAN WAIT ☐ 44 HERE COMES MR
JORDAN ☐ 45 THE VIP'S ☐ 46 ROSE OF WASHING-
TON SQUARE ☐ 47 NOW VOYAGER ☐ 48 MR
SKEFFINGTON ☐ 49 ACROSS THE PACIFIC ☐
50 CASABLANCA ☐
Your score out of a possible 50 :

BLESS THESE HOUSES

1 HOUSE OF DRACULA ☐ 2 A HOUSE IS NOT A
HOME ☐ 3 THE HOUSE OF SEVEN HAWKS ☐ (the
original novel was called THE HOUSE OF SEVEN FLIES)
4 HOUSE ON HAUNTED HILL ☐ 5 THE HOUSE ON
GREENAPPLE ROAD (pilot series for DAN AUGUST) ☐
6 HOUSE OF WAX ☐ 7 THE HOUSE ON 92nd
STREET ☐ 8 HOUSE OF STRANGERS ☐ 9 HOUSE
OF BAMBOO ☐ 10 HOUSE OF CARDS
Your score out of a possible 10 :

LADDERGRAM 8

DALE TREMONT is GINGER ROGERS ☐ in TOP
    HAT ☐
war correspondent CARY GRANT ☐ ONCE UPON A
    HONEYMOON ☐
Indian CORNEL WILDE ☐ IT HAD TO BE YOU ☐
railroad magnate WARREN WILLIAM ☐ UPPER-
    WORLD ☐
D.A. RONALD REAGAN ☐ STORM WARNING ☐
botany professor JAMES STEWART ☐ VIVACIOUS
    LADY ☐

law enforcer EDWARD G. ROBINSON ☐ TIGHT
SPOT ☐
possible spouse GEORGE MURPHY ☐ TOM DICK AND
HARRY ☐
Clay Dalzell WILLIAM POWELL ☐ STAR OF MID-
NIGHT ☐
juror DENNIS MORGAN ☐ PERFECT STRANGERS/
TOO DANGEROUS TO LOVE ☐
shell-shocked war veteran JOSEPH COTTEN ☐ I'LL BE
SEEING YOU ☐
war correspondent WALTER PIDGEON ☐ WEEKEND
AT THE WALDORF ☐
psychiatrist FRED ASTAIRE ☐ CAREFREE ☐

THE ADVENTURES OF . . . WHO?

1 Crime Doctor ☐   2 Philo Vance ☐   3 Charlie Chan ☐
4 The Bowery Boys ☐   5 Michael Shayne ☐   6 Matt
Helm ☐ 7 Jungle Jim ☐ 8 The Lone Wolf ☐ 9 Blondie ☐
10 Lassie ☐   11 Dr Gillespie ☐   12 The Cisco Kid ☐
13 The Hardy Family ☐   14 Sherlock Holmes ☐   15 The
Three Mesquirteers ☐   16 Dr Christian ☐   17 Carry on ☐
18 Mr Wong ☐   19 James Bond ☐   20 Bulldog Drummond
☐
Your score out of a possible 20:

MATCHED PAIRS

1 Annabella ☐ William Powell ☐   2 Hedy Lamarr ☐
Robert Walker ☐   3 Clint Eastwood ☐ Jeff Bridges ☐
4 Barbara Eden ☐ David Hartman ☐   5 Johnny Weiss-
muller ☐ Aquanetta ☐   6 Max Baer ☐ Myrna Loy ☐
7 Clark Gable ☐ Marion Davies ☐ 8 Gene Kelly ☐ Fred
Astaire ☐ 9 Douglass Montgomery ☐ Paulette Goddard ☐
10 Anna Sten ☐ Robert Webber ☐   11 Gary Cooper ☐
Merle Oberon ☐   12 Jeanne Crain ☐ Thelma Ritter ☐
13 James Caan ☐ Alan Arkin ☐   14 Cesar Romero ☐

247

Marjorie Weaver ☐ 15 Ray Milland ☐ Ginger Rogers ☐
16 Deborah Kerr ☐ William Holden ☐ 17 Melina
Mercouri ☐ Keith Michell ☐ 18 Laurence Olivier ☐ Greer
Garson ☐ 19 Billy and Bobby Mauch ☐☐ 20 Glenn
Ford ☐ Gloria de Haven ☐
Your score out of a possible 40 :

FLYNN OF BURMA

1 AGAINST ALL FLAGS ☐ 2 KIM ☐ 3 CRY
WOLF ☐ 4 NEVER SAY GOODBYE ☐ 5 SAN
ANTONIO ☐ 6 UNCERTAIN GLORY ☐ 7 NORTH-
ERN PURSUIT ☐ 8 EDGE OF DARKNESS ☐ 9 DIVE
BOMBER ☐ 10 FOOTSTEPS IN THE DARK ☐
11 THE SEA HAWK ☐ 12 VIRGINIA CITY ☐ 13 THE
DAWN PATROL ☐ 14 THE PRINCE AND THE
PAUPER ☐ 15 THE CASE OF THE CURIOUS
BRIDE ☐
Your score out of a possible 15 :

EGO

1 Ann Dvorak ☐ 2 Barbara Bel Geddes ☐ 3 Cary
Grant ☐ 4 Wendy Hiller ☐ 5 Michael Landon ☐ 6 Susan
Hayward ☐ 7 Claudette Colbert ☐ 8 Gloria Talbot ☐
9 Fredric March ☐ 10 Edward G. Robinson ☐ 11 Ronald
Colman ☐ 12 Laurence Harvey ☐ 13 Susan Hayward ☐
14 Edward G. Robinson ☐ 15 Lilian Harvey ☐
Your score out of a possible 15 :

WOMEN!

1 Miriam Hopkins ☐ 2 Eleanor Parker ☐ 3 Sophia
Loren ☐ 4 Katharine Hepburn ☐ 5 Joan Bennett ☐
6 Bette Davis ☐ 7 Joan Bennett ☐ 8 Ann Sheridan ☐
9 Ida Lupino ☐ 10 Brenda Marshall ☐ 11 Carole
Lombard ☐ 12 Yvonne Mitchell ☐ 13 Virginia Bruce ☐
14 Gale Sondergaard ☐ 15 Barbara Stanwyck ☐ 16 Jean

Harlow ☐ 17 Anna Sten ☐ 18 Miriam Hopkins ☐ 19 Jean
Kent ☐ 20 Joan Crawford ☐
Your score out of a possible 20 :

LADDERGRAM 9

STANLEY TIMBERLAKE is BETTE DAVIS ☐ in IN
    THIS OUR LIFE ☐
small town doctor GEORGE BARBIER ☐ THE MAN
    WHO CAME TO DINNER ☐
Irish horse-trainer HUMPHREY BOGART ☐ DARK
    VICTORY ☐
cousin George WALTER ABEL ☐ MR SKEFFING-
    TON ☐
exasperated employer MONTY WOOLLEY ☐ THE MAN
    WHO CAME TO DINNER ☐
defence lawyer JAMES STEPHENSON ☐ THE
    LETTER ☐
paranoiac composer CLAUDE RAINS ☐ DECEPTION ☐
deceived spouse HERBERT MARSHALL ☐ THE
    LITTLE FOXES or the LETTER ☐
lady in waiting OLIVIA DE HAVILLAND ☐ THE
    PRIVATE LIVES OF ELIZABETH AND ESSEX ☐
cigarette lighter PAUL HENREID ☐ NOW
    VOYAGER ☐
nagging mother GLADYS COOPER ☐ NOW
    VOYAGER ☐
Your score out of a possible 22 :

BETTER KNOWN AS

1 Blondie ☐   2 The Lone Wolf ☐   3 The Thin Man –
though the description actually applies to a character murdered in the first film of the series ☐ 4 The Crime Doctor ☐
5 Mexican Spitfire ☐ 6 The Wolf Man ☐ 7 Doctor in the
House (etc) ☐ 8 Batman ☐
Your score out of a possible 8 :

THE FILM AND THE FACE

1 WHITE HEAT ☐ James Cagney ☐ 2 I MARRIED A WITCH ☐ Fredric March ☐ 3 THE LADY IN THE LAKE ☐ Audrey Totter ☐ 4 PHANTOM OF THE OPERA ☐ Claude Rains ☐ 5 THE THIRD MAN ☐ Joseph Cotten ☐ 6 DOUBLE INDEMNITY ☐ Fred MacMurray ☐ 7 CIMARRON ☐ Richard Dix ☐ 8 A BILL OF DIVORCEMENT ☐ Katharine Hepburn ☐ 9 THE SCARLET PIMPERNEL ☐ Leslie Howard ☐ 10 ALL THIS AND HEAVEN TOO ☐ Bette Davis ☐ 11 SCARFACE ☐ Paul Muni ☐ 12 THE MALTESE FALCON ☐ Mary Astor ☐ 13 LITTLE CAESAR ☐ Edward G. Robinson ☐ 14 ARSENIC AND OLD LACE ☐ Cary Grant ☐ 15 BLITHE SPIRIT ☐ Rex Harrison ☐ 16 PRIDE AND PREJUDICE ☐ Greer Garson ☐ 17 MR SMITH GOES TO WASHINGTON ☐ James Stewart ☐ 18 ANIMAL CRACKERS ☐ Groucho Marx ☐ 19 CITIZEN KANE ☐ Joseph Cotten ☐ 20 THE SIGN OF THE CROSS ☐ Fredric March ☐ 21 THE LITTLE FOXES ☐ Bette Davis ☐ 22 THE GRAPES OF WRATH ☐ Henry Fonda ☐ 23 SATURDAY NIGHT AND SUNDAY MORNING ☐ Albert Finney ☐ 24 SUDDENLY LAST SUMMER ☐ Katharine Hepburn ☐ 25 IT'S A GIFT ☐ W. C. Fields ☐
Your score out of a possible 50:

NOT SO FUNNY

1 Harold Lloyd ☐ 2 Abbott and Costello ☐ 3 Laurel and Hardy ☐ 4 Norman Wisdom ☐ 5 Charlie Chaplin ☐ 6 Buster Keaton ☐ 7 Jack Benny ☐ 8 Danny Kaye ☐ 9 Will Hay ☐ 10 W. C. Fields ☐ 11 Gracie Fields ☐ 12 Olsen and Johnson ☐ 13 Max Miller ☐ 14 Martha Raye ☐ 15 Bob Hope ☐ 16 Eddie Cantor ☐ 17 Jerry Lewis ☐ 18 George Formby ☐ 19 Joe E. Brown ☐ 20 The Ritz Brothers ☐
Your score out of a possible 20:

Answer to POSTER 9: RAWHIDE ☐

LADDERGRAM 10

HARRY VAN is CLARK GABLE ☐ in IDIOT'S
  DELIGHT ☐
singer JEANETTE MACDONALD ☐ SAN
  FRANCISCO ☐
seaman BURT LANCASTER ☐ RUN SILENT RUN
  DEEP ☐
teacher DORIS DAY ☐ TEACHER'S PET ☐
oil man SPENCER TRACY ☐ BOOM TOWN ☐
Judge Cotton FRANK MORGAN ☐ HONKY TONK ☐
procrastinator VIVIEN LEIGH ☐ GONE WITH THE
  WIND ☐
anthropologist's wife GRACE KELLY ☐ MOGAMBO ☐
Susan GRETA GARBO ☐ SUSAN LENOX – HER
  FALL AND RISE ☐
divorcee MARILYN MONROE ☐ THE MISFITS ☐
fellow hitchhiker CLAUDETTE COLBERT ☐ IT HAP-
  PENED ONE NIGHT ☐
Your score out of possible 22:

THE MURDERER IS IN THIS ROOM

1 Rosamund John ☐ 2 James Stewart ☐ 3 Mary Astor ☐
4 Clifton Webb ☐ 5 George Brent ☐ 6 Robert Ryan ☐
7 Lloyd Nolan ☐ 8 Kirk Douglas ☐ 9 Gerald Hamer ☐
10 Lowell Gilmore ☐ 11 Arthur Hill ☐ 12 Barry Fitzgerald ☐ 13 Richard Carlson ☐ 14 H. B. Warner ☐
15 Douglass Montgomery ☐ 16 Cesar Romero ☐ 17 Ralph
Morgan ☐ 18 Elisha Cook Jnr ☐ 19 Jean Arthur ☐ 20 Ted
De Corsia ☐ 21 Tyrone Power ☐ 22 Nobody actually murders anybody, though Ray Milland hires Anthony Dawson
to do one for him. Dawson is killed in self-defence by Grace
Kelly ☐ 23 Laird Cregar ☐ 24 Richard Todd ☐ 25 Barry
Foster ☐
Your score out of a possible 25:

251

FREDERIC IS COMPOSING TONIGHT

1 RHAPSODY IN BLUE ☐ George Gershwin ☐
2 NIGHT AND DAY ☐ Cole Porter ☐ 3 SONG OF
LOVE ☐ Johannes Brahms ☐ 4 SONG OF SHEHEREZ-
ADE ☐ Nikolai Rimsky-Korsakoff ☐ 5 SONG WITHOUT
END ☐ Franz Liszt ☐ 6 MAGIC FIRE ☐ Richard
Wagner ☐ 7 SONG OF LOVE ☐ Robert Schumann ☐
8 BLOSSOM TIME ☐ Franz Schubert ☐ 9 THE GREAT
MR HANDEL ☐ George Frederick Handel ☐ 10 THE
STORY OF GILBERT AND SULLIVAN ☐ Arthur
Sullivan ☐ 11 ST LOUIS BLUES ☐ W. C. Handy ☐
12 DEEP IN MY HEART ☐ Sigmund Romberg ☐
13 THE MUSIC LOVERS ☐ Peter Tchaikovsky ☐
14 LA SYMPHONIE FANTASTIQUE ☐ Hector
Berlioz ☐ 15 THE GREAT WALTZ ☐ Johann Strauss ☐
16 THE GREAT VICTOR HERBERT ☐ Victor
Herbert ☐ 17 TILL THE CLOUDS ROLL BY ☐ Jerome
Kern ☐ 18 SWANEE RIVER ☐ Stephen Foster ☐
19 SONG OF NORWAY ☐ Edvard Grieg ☐ 20 THE
BEST THINGS IN LIFE ARE FREE ☐ De Sylva ☐
Brown ☐ and Henderson ☐ 21 THREE LITTLE
WORDS ☐ Bert Kalmar ☐ and Harry Ruby ☐ 22 MY
GAL SAL ☐ Paul Dresser ☐ 23 WORDS AND
MUSIC ☐ Richard Rodgers ☐ Lorenx Hart ☐ 24 STARS
AND STRIPES FOREVER (GB: MARCHING
ALONG) ☐ John Philip Sousa ☐ 25 THE MAGNIFI-
CENT REBEL ☐ Ludwig Van Beethoven ☐
Your score out of a possible 54 :

OH, JOHNNY, OH

1 Henry Silva ☐ 2 Sterling Hayden ☐ 3 Dick Powell ☐
4 Frank Sinatra ☐ 5 Tony Curtis ☐ 6 James Cagney ☐
7 George Raft ☐ 8 Robert Taylor ☐ 9 Hal Stalmaster ☐
10 Peter Finch ☐
Your score out of a possible 10 :

LADDERGRAM 11

SIR HUGH MARCY is RAY MILLAND ☐ in KITTY ☐
brother PHILIP TERRY ☐ THE LOST WEEKEND ☐
native DOROTHY LAMOUR ☐ THE JUNGLE PRIN-
   CESS or HER JUNGLE LOVE ☐
diver JOHN WAYNE ☐ REAP THE WILD WIND ☐
politician THOMAS MITCHELL ☐ ALIAS NICK
   BEAL ☐
gypsy MARLENE DIETRICH ☐ GOLDEN EAR-
   RINGS ☐
intended victim GRACE KELLY ☐ DIAL M FOR
   MURDER ☐
villain CHARLES LAUGHTON ☐ THE BIG
   CLOCK ☐
nurse FRANK FAYLEN ☐ THE LOST WEEKEND ☐
lover RYAN O'NEAL ☐ LOVE STORY ☐
journalist CLAUDETTE COLBERT ☐ ARISE MY
   LOVE ☐
Your score out of a possible 22 :

MORE THAN ONE TALENT

1 Walter Matthau ☐   2 Dick Powell ☐   3 Charles Laughton ☐   4 Richard Haydn ☐   5 Lionel Jeffries ☐   6 John
Mills ☐ 7 Lionel Barrymore ☐ 8 Karl Malden ☐ 9 James
Cagney ☐   10 Roddy MacDowall ☐   11 Clint Eastwood ☐
12 Peter Lorre ☐   13 Albert Finney ☐   14 Ray Milland ☐
15 Gene Kelly ☐   16 Robert Montgomery ☐   17 David
Hemmings ☐   18 Charlton Heston ☐   19 Clive Brook ☐
20 Jack Lemmon ☐   21 Sidney Poitier ☐   22 Mickey
Rooney ☐ 23 Richard Attenborough ☐ 24 Martin Gabel ☐
25 Mel Ferrer ☐   26 Jose Ferrer ☐   27 Alan Arkin ☐
28 Paul Newman ☐   29 Paul Henried ☐   30 Burt
Lancaster ☐   31 Frank Sinatra ☐   32 Edmond O'Brien ☐
33 Ralph Richardson ☐   34 Cornel Wilde ☐   35 Laurence
Harvey ☐
Your score out of a possible 35 :

THEY SUFFERED A SEA CHANGE II

1 THE WAY AHEAD ☐   2 A TOWN LIKE ALICE ☐
3 THE QUATERMASS EXPERIMENT ☐   4 THE
STORY OF ESTHER COSTELLO ☐ 5 A MATTER OF
LIFE AND DEATH ☐   6 CRY THE BELOVED
COUNTRY ☐ 7 BUSMAN'S HONEYMOON ☐ 8 THE
CARD ☐   9 FANATIC ☐   10 THE FIRST OF THE
FEW ☐   11 PIMPERNEL SMITH ☐ 12 THE WAY TO
THE STARS ☐   13 WITCHFINDER GENERAL ☐
14 YOUNG AND INNOCENT ☐   15 SABOTAGE ☐
16 WHISKY GALORE ☐   17 ICE COLD IN ALEX ☐
18 FANNY BY GASLIGHT ☐ 19 FATHER BROWN ☐
20 THE BATTLE OF THE RIVER PLATE ☐
Your score out of a possible 20:

DEAR MR GABLE

1 NO MAN OF HER OWN ☐ 2 CAIN AND MABEL ☐
3 STRANGE CARGO ☐   4 ACROSS THE WIDE
MISSOURI ☐   5 HOMECOMING ☐   6 ADVEN-
TURE ☐   7 THE PAINTED DESERT ☐   8 IT HAP-
PENED ONE NIGHT ☐ 9 CHINA SEAS ☐ 10 SAN
FRANCISCO ☐   11 IDIOT'S DELIGHT ☐ 12 PAR-
NELL ☐ 13 COMRADE X ☐ NEVER LET ME GO ☐
14 TOO HOT TO HANDLE ☐   15 THE HUCKSTERS
☐ 16 KEY TO THE CITY ☐   17 LONE STAR ☐
18 BUT NOT FOR ME ☐ (a remake of ACCENT ON
YOUTH and MR MUSIC) 19 THEY MET IN BOMBAY
☐ 20 THE WHITE SISTER ☐
Your score out of a possible 21:

THE TOPIC IS BIOPICS

1 Carole Lombard ☐ GABLE AND LOMBARD ☐
2 Texas Guinan ☐ INCENDIARY BLONDE ☐   3 Otis

Skinner ☐ OUR HEARTS WERE YOUNG AND GAY ☐
4 David Garrick ☐ THE GREAT GARRICK ☐ 5 Jean
Harlow ☐ HARLOW ☐ 6 Mrs Leslie Carter ☐ LADY
WITH RED HAIR ☐ 7 Eddie Cantor ☐ THE EDDIE
CANTOR STORY ☐ 8 Edwin Booth ☐ PRINCE OF
PLAYERS ☐ 9 Lillian Roth ☐ I'LL CRY TOMOR-
ROW ☐ 10 Buster Keaton ☐ THE BUSTER KEATON
STORY ☐ 11 John Barrymore ☐ TOO MUCH TOO
SOON ☐ 12 Red Nichols ☐ THE FIVE PENNIES ☐
13 W. C. Fields ☐ W. C. FIELDS AND ME ☐ 14 Jeanne
Eagels ☐ JEANNE EAGELS ☐ 15 Lon Chaney ☐ MAN
OF A THOUSAND FACES ☐ 16 Pearl White ☐ THE
PERILS OF PAULINE ☐ 17 Houdini ☐ HOUDINI ☐
18 Lillian Russell ☐ LILLIAN RUSSELL ☐ 19 Ruth
Etting ☐ LOVE ME OR LEAVE ME ☐ 20 Marilyn
Miller ☐ LOOK FOR THE SILVER LINING ☐ 21 The
Dolly Sisters ☐ THE DOLLY SISTERS ☐ 22 George
Leybourne ☐ CHAMPAGNE CHARLIE ☐ 23 Gene
Krupa ☐ THE GENE KRUPA STORY (GB: DRUM
CRAZY) ☐ 24 Helen Morgan ☐ THE HELEN MORGAN
STORY (GB: BOTH ENDS OF THE CANDLE) ☐
25 Nellie Melba ☐ MELBA ☐ 26 Nora Bayes ☐ SHINE
ON HARVEST MOON ☐ 27 Blossom Seeley ☐ SOME-
BODY LOVES ME ☐ 28 Gypsy Rose Lee ☐ GYPSY ☐
29 Billie Holliday ☐ LADY SINGS THE BLUES ☐
30 Joe E. Lewis ☐ THE JOKER IS WILD ☐
Your score out of a possible 60:

SILENCE PLEASE II

1 Pola Negri ☐ 2 Squibs ☐ 3 JOYLESS STREET ☐
4 THE BATTLESHIP POTEMKIN ☐ 5 BERLIN ☐
6 THE LODGER ☐ 7 SHOOTING STARS ☐ 8 UN
CHIEN ANDALOU ☐ 9 SIR ARNE'S TREASURE ☐
10 WITCHCRAFT THROUGH THE AGES ☐ 11 Emil
Jannings ☐ 12 VARIETY or VAUDEVILLE ☐ 13 THE
STUDENT OF PRAGUE ☐ 14 METROPOLIS ☐

15 THE LOVES OF JEANNE NEY ☐ 16 Falconetti ☐
17 NAPOLEON ☐   18 Carl Mayer ☐ and Hans
Janowitz ☐ 19 THE SEASHELL AND THE CLERGY-
MAN ☐ 20 Rene Clair ☐
Your score out of a possible 21 :

LADDERGRAM 12

RALPH COTTER is JAMES CAGNEY ☐ in KISS
   TOMORROW GOODBYE ☐
king VICTOR JORY ☐ A MIDSUMMER NIGHT'S
   DREAM ☐
soldier DAN DAILEY ☐ WHAT PRICE GLORY ☐
   FBI EDMOND O'BRIEN ☐ WHITE HEAT ☐
stranded entertainer ANN SHERIDAN ☐ TORRID
   ZONE ☐
Ruth DORIS DAY ☐ LOVE ME OR LEAVE ME ☐
Moll MAE CLARKE ☐ PUBLIC ENEMY ☐
tycoon's daughter BETTE DAVIS ☐ THE BRIDE CAME
   C O D ☐
alcoholic GIG YOUNG ☐ COME FILL THE CUP ☐
lieutenant HENRY FONDA ☐ MISTER ROBERTS ☐
vaudevillian WALTER HUSTON ☐ YANKEE DOODLE
   DANDY ☐
dancer RUBY KEELER ☐ FOOTLIGHT PARADE ☐
Your score out of a posible 24 :

LADDERGRAM 13

OWEN THURSDAY is HENRY FONDA ☐ in FORT
   APACHE ☐
old actor HERBERT MARSHALL ☐ STAGE
   STRUCK ☐
male impersonator ANNABELLA ☐ WINGS OF THE
   MORNING ☐
con woman GENE TIERNEY ☐ RINGS ON HER
   FINGERS ☐

famous "doctor" VICTOR MATURE (Doc Holliday) ☐
   MY DARLING CLEMENTINE ☐
murderer TONY CURTIS ☐ THE BOSTON STRANG-
   LER ☐
Daisy JOAN CRAWFORD ☐ DAISY KENYON ☐
doctor WILLIAM POWELL ☐ MISTER ROBERTS ☐
inventor DON AMECHE ☐ THE STORY OF ALEX-
   ANDER GRAHAM BELL ☐
western wife JOANNE WOODWARD ☐ A BIG HAND
   FOR THE LITTLE LADY ☐
ex-president LEE TRACY ☐ THE BEST MAN ☐
Your score out of a possible 22 :

COLOURS OF THE RAINBOW

1 pink ☐   2 red ☐   3 white ☐   4 red ☐   5 blue ☐
6 yellow ☐   7 purple ☐   8 pink ☐   9 black ☐   10 white ☐
11 red ☐   12 green ☐   13 crimson ☐   14 scarlet ☐   15 red ☐
16 slightly ☐   17 bride ☐   18 bride ☐   19 reflections ☐
20 lady ☐   21 woman ☐   22 man ☐   23 gold ☐
24 woman ☐   25 hot ☐   26 forever ☐   27 perfect ☐
28 babies ☐   29 gabriel ☐   30 water ☐   death ☐
Your score out of a possible 31 :

DEBUTANTES

1 Shirley Temple ☐   2 Clark Gable ☐   3 Fred MacMurray
☐ (THE GILDED LILY was released first.)   4 Rock
Hudson ☐   5 James Mason ☐   6 Jane Fonda ☐   7 Spencer
Tracy ☐ 8 Peter Fonda ☐ 9 William Holden ☐ 10 Frank
Sinatra ☐   11 Kirk Douglas ☐   12 Dorothy McGuire ☐
13 Sidney Greenstreet ☐   14 Mae West ☐   15 Glenn
Ford ☐ 16 Shirley MacLaine ☐ 17 John Garfield ☐ 18 Yul
Brynner ☐   19 Gene Kelly ☐   20 Charlton Heston ☐
21 Claude Rains ☐   22 Sidney Poitier ☐   23 Humphrey
Bogart ☐ 24 Burt Lancaster ☐ 25 Dirk Bogarde ☐ 26 Cary

Grant ☐   27 Raymond Massey ☐   28 Edith Evans ☐
29 Elizabeth Taylor ☐   30 Bette Davis ☐
Your score out of a possible 30:

UNLIKELY BEHAVIOUR

1 THE GHOUL ☐ 2 REBECCA ☐ (at a fancy dress ball)
3 THE ADVENTURES OF SHERLOCK HOLMES ☐
4 GENGHIS KHAN ☐ 5 AFTER THE THIN MAN ☐
6 NIGHT TRAIN TO MUNICH ☐ 7 THE SCARLET
PIMPERNEL ☐   8 THE DEVIL DOLL ☐   9 THE
KREMLIN LETTER ☐ 10 HOUSE OF DRACULA ☐
11 THE GREAT PROFILE ☐ 12 THE BLUE BIRD ☐
(and vice versa)   13 BREAKFAST AT TIFFANY'S ☐
14 FOREIGN CORRESPONDENT ☐ 15 THE RETURN
OF DR X ☐ 16 BLONDE VENUS ☐ 17 GORILLA AT
LARGE ☐ 18 THE GREAT LOVER ☐ 19 HOLLY-
WOOD CAVALCADE ☐ 20 ABBOTT AND COSTELLO
MEET DR JEKYLL AND MR HYDE ☐ 21 THE LOST
MOMENT ☐   22 MY MAN GODFREY (1936) ☐
23 NOTHING SACRED ☐ 24 THE HOUSEKEEPER'S
DAUGHTER ☐ 25 SUMMERTIME/ SUMMER MAD-
NESS ☐   26 SULLIVAN'S TRAVELS ☐   27 THE
MIRACLE OF MORGAN'S CREEK ☐ 28 THE LADY
VANISHES ☐ 29 THE STORY OF MANKIND (Peter
Minuit) ☐ 30 SAN DIEGO I LOVE YOU ☐
Your score out of a possible 30:

Answer to POSTER 11: THE GARDEN OF ALLAH ☐

HUMBLE BEGINNINGS

1 Yul Brynner ☐ THE KING AND I ☐   2 Monty
Woolley ☐ THE MAN WHO CAME TO DINNER ☐
3 Joseph Cotten ☐ CITIZEN KANE ☐ 4 Clifton Webb ☐
LAURA ☐   5 Sidney Greenstreet ☐   THE MALTESE
FALCON ☐ 6 Peter Lorre ☐ M ☐ 7 Claude Rains ☐

THE INVISIBLE MAN ☐ 8 Albert Finney ☐ SATUR-
DAY NIGHT AND SUNDAY MORNING ☐ 9 Stephen
Boyd ☐ THE MAN WHO NEVER WAS ☐ 10 Marlene
Dietrich ☐ THE BLUE ANGEL ☐ 11 Red Skelton ☐
WHISTLING IN THE DARK ☐ 12 Alan Ladd ☐ THIS
GUN FOR HIRE ☐

Your score out of a possible 24 :

OLD NICK

1 Alan Mowbray ☐ 2 Jules Berry ☐ 3 Rex Ingram ☐
4 Laird Cregar ☐ 5 Claude Rains ☐ 6 Vincent Price ☐
7 Ray Walston ☐ 8 Ralph Richardson ☐ 9 Walter
Huston ☐ 10 Stanley Holloway ☐ 11 Adolphe Menjou ☐
12 Ray Milland ☐

Your score out of a possible 12 :

FATEFUL MEETINGS

1 Veronica Lake ☐ Alan Ladd ☐ THIS GUN FOR
HIRE ☐ 2 Gloria Swanson ☐ William Holden ☐ SUN-
SET BOULEVARD ☐ 3 Veronica Lake ☐ Fredric
March ☐ I MARRIED A WITCH ☐ 4 Mary Astor ☐
Walter Huston ☐ DODSWORTH ☐ 5 Greta Garbo ☐
Melvyn Douglas ☐ NINOTCHKA ☐ 6 Dorothy Coming-
ore ☐ Orson Welles ☐ CITIZEN KANE ☐ 7 Marlene
Dietrich ☐ James Stewart ☐ DESTRY RIDES AGAIN ☐
8 Eva Marie Saint ☐ Cary Grant ☐ NORTH BY NORTH-
WEST ☐ 9 Katharine Hepburn ☐ James Stewart ☐ THE
PHILADELPHIA STORY ☐ 10 Greer Garson ☐
Laurence Olivier ☐ PRIDE AND PREJUDICE ☐ 11 Joan
Fontaine ☐ Laurence Olivier ☐ REBECCA ☐ 12 Veronica
Lake ☐ Joel McCrea ☐ SULLIVAN'S TRAVELS ☐

Your score out of a possible 36 :

YOU DIRTY RAT

1 ANGELS WITH DIRTY FACES ☐ 2 CAPTAINS OF THE CLOUDS ☐ 3 TORRID ZONE ☐ 4 FOOTLIGHT PARADE ☐ 5 HARD TO HANDLE ☐ 6 THE TIME OF YOUR LIFE ☐ 7 NEVER STEAL ANYTHING SMALL ☐ 8 13 RUE MADELEINE ☐ 9 JOHNNY COME LATELY ☐ 10 THE BRIDE CAME C. O. D. ☐ 11 THE STRAWBERRY BLONDE ☐ 12 THE FIGHTING 69th ☐ 13 BOY MEETS GIRL ☐ 14 SMART MONEY ☐ 15 LADY KILLER ☐

Your score out of a possible 15:

Answer to POSTER 12: BILLION DOLLAR BRAIN ☐

WHO NEEDS *TWO* STARS?

1 Burt Lancaster ☐ Jean Peters ☐ 2 Ava Gardner ☐ Anthony Franciosa ☐ 3 John Barrymore ☐ Mary Astor ☐ 4 Al Jolson ☐ Betty Bronson ☐ 5 Marlene Dietrich ☐ John Lodge ☐ 6 Ramon Novarro ☐ May McAvoy ☐ 7 Charlton Heston ☐ Haya Harareet ☐ 8 Lillian Gish ☐ Lars Hanson ☐ 9 Barbara Stanwyck ☐ John Boles ☐ 10 Clark Gable ☐ Maria Elena Marques ☐ 11 Errol Flynn ☐ Brenda Marshall ☐ 12 Clara Bow ☐ Antonio Moreno ☐ 13 Katharine Hepburn ☐ John Beal ☐ 14 John Wayne ☐ Nancy Olson ☐ 15 Spencer Tracy ☐ Signe Hasso ☐ 16 Humphrey Bogart ☐ Irene Manning ☐ 17 Susan Hayward ☐ Michael Connors ☐ 18 Greta Garbo ☐ Ramon Novarro ☐ 19 David Niven ☐ Olivia de Havilland ☐ 20 Gary Cooper ☐ Teresa Wright ☐ 21 Ronald Colman ☐ Anna Lee ☐ 22 Danny Kaye ☐ Mai Zetterling ☐ 24 James Cagney ☐ Joan Leslie ☐ 25 Joel McCrea ☐ Laraine Day ☐

Your score out of a possible 50:

TRIPLE TROUBLE I

1 THREE CORNERED MOON ☐ 2 THREE DARING DAUGHTERS ☐ 3 THREE COINS IN THE FOUNTAIN ☐ 4 THREE BLIND MICE ☐ 5 THREE STRIPES IN THE SUN ☐ 6 THREE STRANGERS ☐ 7 THREE CAME HOME ☐ 8 THREE BRAVE MEN ☐ 9 THREE SMART GIRLS ☐ 10 THREE MEN IN WHITE ☐ 11 THREE LITTLE WORDS ☐ 12 THREE INTO TWO WON'T GO ☐ 13 THREE MEN ON A HORSE ☐ 14 THREE-TEN TO YUMA ☐

Your score out of a possible 14:

LADDERGRAM 14

J. J. BEALLER is CHARLES LAUGHTON ☐ in THE BRIBE ☐

fugitive FREDRIC MARCH ☐ LES MISERABLES ☐

missionary ELSA LANCHESTER ☐ VESSEL OF WRATH / THE BEACHCOMBER ☐

wife BINNIE BARNES ☐ THE PRIVATE LIFE OF HENRY VIII ☐

servant BORIS KARLOFF ☐ THE STRANGE DOOR ☐

slave KIRK DOUGLAS ☐ SPARTACUS ☐

gypsy MAUREEN O'HARA ☐ THE HUNCHBACK OF NOTRE DAME ☐

daughter NORMA SHEARER ☐ THE BARRETTS OF WIMPOLE STREET ☐

dancer VIVIEN LEIGH ☐ ST MARTIN'S LANE / SIDEWALKS OF LONDON ☐

wife GERTRUDE LAWRENCE ☐ REMBRANDT ☐

employer CHARLES RUGGLES ☐ RUGGLES OF RED GAP ☐

naval officer CLARK GABLE ☐ MUTINY ON THE BOUNTY ☐

host ERNEST THESIGER ☐ THE OLD DARK HOUSE ☐

bather CLAUDETTE COLBERT ☐ THE SIGN OF THE CROSS ☐

dancer RITA HAYWORTH ☐ SALOME ☐

bootmaker JOHN MILLS ☐ HOBSON'S CHOICE ☐

Your score out of a possible 32:

THE FAMILY HOUR

1 Ray Milland ☐ 2 Gladys Cooper ☐ 3 Thomas Mitchell ☐ 4 May Robson ☐ 5 Edna May Oliver ☐ 6 Susan Kohner ☐ 7 Henry Fonda ☐ 8 Janet Blair ☐ 9 Marjorie Main ☐ 10 Walter Pidgeon ☐ 11 Virginia Mayo ☐ 12 Murray Hamilton ☐ 13 Adolphe Menjou ☐ 14 John Halliday ☐ 15 Mary Boland ☐ 16 Ann Blyth ☐ 17 Una O'Connor ☐ 18 Ann Dvorak ☐ 19 Elizabeth Taylor ☐ 20 Ruth Chatterton ☐ 21 Nigel Bruce ☐ 22 Bobs Watson ☐ 23 Luise Rainer ☐ 24 Brian Aherne ☐ 25 John Howard ☐ 26 Doris Nolan ☐ 27 Gloria Stuart ☐ 28 Diana Lynn ☐ 29 Cyril Raymond ☐ 30 Harry Shannon ☐ 31 Josephine Hull ☐ 32 Eva Moore ☐ Brember Wills ☐ John Dudgeon (actually Elspeth Dudgeon) ☐ 33 Warner Oland ☐ 34 Mae Busch ☐ 35 Geraldine Fitzgerald ☐ 36 Helen Broderick ☐ 37 Roland Young ☐ 38 Alan Hale ☐ 39 Betty Field ☐ 40 Robert Warwick ☐ 41 Jane Darwell ☐ 42 Billie Whitelaw ☐ 43 Harry Davenport ☐ 44 Michael Redgrave ☐ 45 Spring Byington ☐ 46 Sara Haden ☐ 47 Tim Holt ☐ 48 Frederick Kerr ☐ 49 Alice Brady ☐ 50 Charles Coburn ☐ 51 Teresa Wright ☐ 52 Maggie Smith ☐

Your score out of a possible 54:

Answer to POSTER 13: WALK ON THE WILD SIDE

MORE STARS THAN THERE ARE IN THE SKY

1 SHOW OF SHOWS ☐ 2 STAR SPANGLED RHYTHM ☐ 3 THANK YOUR LUCKY STARS ☐ 4 ZEIG-

FELD FOLLIES ☐ 5 PARAMOUNT ON PARADE ☐ 6 KING OF JAZZ ☐ 7 STAR SPANGLED RHYTHM ☐ 8 HOLLYWOOD REVUE OF 1929 ☐ 9 FOLLOW THE BOYS ☐ 10 THANK YOUR LUCKY STARS ☐
Your score out of a possible 10:

FROM THE ORIGINAL NOVEL

1 THE OLD DARK HOUSE ☐ 2 CROSSFIRE ☐ 3 THE RUSSIANS ARE COMING, THE RUSSIANS ARE COMING ☐ 4 THE LADY VANISHES ☐ 5 THE SPIRAL STAIRCASE ☐ 6 A FACE IN THE CROWD ☐ 7 MAN HUNT ☐ 8 THE MARK OF ZORRO ☐ 9 SPELLBOUND ☐ 10 THE BIRTH OF A NATION ☐ 11 VERTIGO ☐ 12 THE SOUTHERNER ☐ 13 JUAREZ ☐ 14 YOUNG AND INNOCENT (THE GIRL WAS YOUNG) ☐ 15 BULLITT ☐ 16 DR STRANGE-LOVE ☐ 17 SUSPICION ☐ 18 JULIA MISBEHAVES ☐ 19 I REMEMBER MAMA ☐ 20 CAMELOT ☐ 21 THE BEST YEARS OF OUR LIVES ☐ 22 TOP-KAPI ☐ 23 TONY ROME ☐ 24 THIS GUN FOR HIRE ☐ 25 STAGE FRIGHT ☐
Your score out of a possible 25:

WORLD GAZETTEER

1 JAMAICA ☐ 2 ARABIA ☐ 3 AMERICA ☐ 4 ALGERIA ☐ 5 SHANGHAI ☐ 6 PARIS ☐ 7 HOLLY-WOOD ☐ 8 CALAIS ☐ 9 MEXICO ☐ 10 BERLIN ☐ 11 MOSCOW ☐ 12 WEST POINT ☐ 13 TAHITI ☐ 14 BRIGHTON ☐ 15 MOSCOW ☐ 16 MUNICH ☐ 17 MADRID ☐ 18 NEW YORK ☐ 19 PARIS ☐ 20 IRELAND ☐ 21 FRISCO ☐ 22 BATAAN ☐ 23 SAN DIEGO ☐ 24 FRISCO ☐ 25 TRINIDAD ☐
Your score out of a possible 25:

ANATOMY

1 TOES ☐ 2 SHOULDER ☐ 3 EYES ☐ 4 SKULL ☐
5 HAND ☐ 6 BRAIN ☐ 7 FINGERS ☐ 8 LIPS ☐
9 THUMB ☐ 10 PALM ☐ 11 FACE ☐ 12 EYES ☐
13 KNEE ☐ 14 LEGS ☐ 15 CLAW ☐ 16 BACK ☐
17 FACE ☐ 18 EYES ☐ 19 HANDS ☐ 20 EYE ☐
21 FACE ☐ 22 HAND ☐ 23 FOOT ☐ 24 EYE ☐
25 HAND ☐
Your score out of a possible 25 :

BIOPICS AGAIN

1 Aviator ☐ REACH FOR THE SKY ☐ Kenneth More ☐
2 Songwriter ☐ I'LL SEE YOU IN MY DREAMS ☐
Danny Thomas ☐ 3 Spy ☐ CARVE HER NAME WITH
PRIDE ☐ Virginia McKenna ☐ 4 Bandleader and
trumpeter ☐ THE FIVE PENNIES ☐ Danny Kaye ☐
5 Entertainer and playwright and songwriter ☐ YANKEE
DOODLE DANDY ☐ James Cagney ☐ 6 King ☐
ALFRED THE GREAT ☐ David Hemmings ☐ 7 Inven-
tor ☐ SO GOES MY LOVE (GB: A GENIUS IN THE
FAMILY) ☐ Don Ameche ☐ 8 Research scientist ☐ THE
STORY OF DR EHRLICH'S MAGIC BULLET ☐
Edward G. Robinson ☐ 9 Baseball player ☐ THE
WINNING TEAM ☐ Ronald Reagan ☐ 10 Inventor ☐
THE STORY OF ALEXANDER GRAHAM BELL ☐
(GB: THE MODERN MIRACLE) Don Ameche ☐
11 Aviatrix ☐ THEY FLEW ALONE (US: WINGS AND
THE WOMAN) ☐ Anna Neagle ☐ 12 Singer ☐ A
LADY'S MORALS ☐ Grace Moore ☐ 13 Singer ☐
WITH A SONG IN MY HEART ☐ Susan Hayward ☐
14 Inventor ☐ THE MAGIC BOX ☐ Robert Donat ☐
15 Actress ☐ PEG OF OLD DRURY ☐ Anna Neagle ☐
16 Singer ☐ THE INTERRUPTED MELODY ☐ Eleanor
Parker ☐ 17 Music hall performer ☐ AFTER THE
BALL ☐ Pat Kirkwood ☐ 18 Aviation pioneer ☐

GALLANT JOURNEY ☐ Glenn Ford ☐ 19 War veteran ☐ HELL TO ETERNITY ☐ Jeffrey Hunter ☐ 20 War correspondent ☐ THE STORY OF GI JOE ☐ Burgess Meredith ☐ 21 Convict ☐ BIRDMAN OF ALCATRAZ ☐ Burt Lancaster ☐ 22 Impresario ☐ TO-NIGHT WE SING ☐ David Wayne ☐ 23 Convicted murderess ☐ I WANT TO LIVE ☐ Susan Hayward ☐ 24 Sailor ☐ JOHN PAUL JONES ☐ Robert Stack ☐ 25 Entertainer ☐ THE I DON'T CARE GIRL ☐ Mitzi Gaynor ☐ 26 Comedian ☐ THE SEVEN LITTLE FOYS ☐ Bob Hope ☐ 27 Aircraft inventor ☐ THE FIRST OF THE FEW ☐ Leslie Howard ☐ 28 Singer ☐ SO THIS IS LOVE ☐ Kathryn Grayson ☐ 29 States-man ☐ A MAN FOR ALL SEASONS ☐ Paul Scofield ☐ 30 Missionary ☐ THE INN OF THE SIXTH HAPPI-NESS ☐ Ingrid Bergman ☐
Your score out of a possible 90:

ACTORS IN COMMON (2 marks per question)

1 They all played the butler in RUGGLES OF RED GAP ☐: in 1923, 1934, and (with variations, as FANCY PANTS) in 1950.

2 They all played DR JEKYLL AND MR HYDE: in 1919, 1960 and 1941 respectively.

3 They all played Death ☐: in 1934 (DEATH TAKES A HOLIDAY), 1938 (ON BORROWED TIME), and 1948 (ORPHEE).

4 They all played members of the Frankenstein family ☐: in FRANKENSTEIN MEETS THE WOLF MAN (1943), GHOST OF FRANKENSTEIN (1941) and SON OF FRANKENSTEIN (1939).

5 They all played opposite Greta Garbo ☐: in NINOT-CHKA (and TWO FACED WOMAN), THE KISS, CONQUEST, FLESH AND THE DEVIL (also LOVE and QUEEN CHRISTINA), and ANNA KARENINA.

6 They all played Abraham Lincoln ☐: in YOUNG MR

LINCOLN (1939), ABE LINCOLN IN ILLINOIS (1940) (also HOW THE WEST WAS WON) and ABRAHAM LINCOLN (1930).

7 They all played Raymond Chandler's private eye Philip Marlowe ☐: in 1947 (THE BRASHER DOUBLOON/THE HIGH WINDOW), 1973 (THE LONG GOODBYE) and 1946 (THE LADY IN THE LAKE).

8 They all played opposite Charles Chaplin ☐: in 1936 (MODERN TIMES) (also 1940, THE GREAT DICTATOR), 1952 (LIMELIGHT), 1947 (MONSIEUR VERDOUX) and 1957 (A KING IN NEW YORK).

9 They all played Catherine the Great of Russia ☐: in 1959 (JOHN PAUL JONES), 1945 (A ROYAL SCANDAL) and 1934 (CATHERINE THE GREAT).

10 They all played the leading roles in Graham Greene adaptations ☐: CONFIDENTIAL AGENT, MINISTRY OF FEAR, THE THIRD MAN, THE FALLEN IDOL, THE HEART OF THE MATTER.

11 They all played dipsomaniacs ☐: in SOMETHING TO LIVE FOR, DAYS OF WINE AND ROSES, SMASH-UP, THE LOST WEEKEND.

12 They all played dual roles ☐: in A STOLEN LIFE, (and DEAD RINGER), THE MASQUERADER (and THE PRISONER OF ZENDA), THE DARK MIRROR, THE CORSICAN BROTHERS.

13 They all played THE HUNCHBACK OF NOTRE DAME ☐: in 1939, 1956, 1923.

14 They all played ELLERY QUEEN in various films of the thirties and forties ☐.

15 They all played MERTON OF THE MOVIES ☐: in 1952, 1932 (as MAKE ME A STAR) and 1923.

16 They all played Professor Moriarty in Sherlock Holmes films ☐: THE TRIUMPH OF SHERLOCK HOLMES, THE ADVENTURES OF SHERLOCK HOLMES, THE WOMAN IN GREEN.

17 They all played THE SCARLET PIMPERNEL ☐: in 1934, 1939 (THE RETURN OF THE SCARLET

PIMPERNEL), and 1951 (THE ELUSIVE PIMPER-
NEL).

18 They all played murderous ladies ☐ in IVY, GREEN
FOR DANGER, HOMICIDAL, and STRAIT JACKET
respectively.

19 They all played Napoleon Bonaparte ☐: in CON-
QUEST, WAR AND PEACE (and others), WATERLOO
repectively.

20 They all played THE PHANTOM OF THE
OPERA ☐: in 1964, 1926, 1943.

21 They all played Anna Leonowens ☐: in ANNA AND
THE KING OF SIAM, ANNA AND THE KING (TV
series), and THE KING AND I.

22 They all played Horatio Nelson ☐: in NELSON, A
BEQUEST TO THE NATION, LADY HAMILTON.

23 They all played Popes ☐: in THE SHOES OF THE
FISHERMAN, BROTHER SUN AND SISTER
MOON, THE AGONY AND THE ECSTASY.

24 They all played Julius Caesar ☐: in CAESAR AND
CLEOPATRA, JULIUS CAESAR (1952), CLEO-
PATRA (1934).

25 They all played John Dillinger ☐ (public enemy number
one in YOUNG DILLINGER, DILLINGER (1945),
DILLINGER (1973).

26 They all played ventriloquists ☐: in KNOCK ON
WOOD, DEAD OF NIGHT, THE GREAT GABBO.

27 They all played The Saint : in the 30s, on TV, and in
the 60s in France.

28 They are all original members of the Dead End Kids ☐.

29 They all played Bulldog Drummond ☐, the first two in
the twenties and thirties, the third more recently in
DEADLIER THAN THE MALE and SOME GIRLS
DO.

30 They all played the Frankenstein monster ☐: at Universal in the forties, at Hammer in the sixties, and in
FRANKENSTEIN MEETS THE WOLF MAN.

Your score out of a possible 60 :

NUMBERS

1 THREE ☐ 2 FIVE ☐ 3 ONE HUNDRED ☐
4 TWENTY-ONE ☐ 5 FOUR ☐ 6 TWO ☐ 7 FIVE ☐
8 SEVEN ☐ 9 FIVE ☐ 10 A THOUSAND AND
ONE ☐ 11 TWO ☐ 12 SIX ☐ 13 TWO ☐
14 THREE ☐ 15 THREE ☐ 16 TWO ☐ 17 THREE ☐
18 FORTY THOUSAND ☐ 19 FOUR 20 FOUR ☐
21 FORTY-FIVE ☐ 22 THREE ☐ 23 FOUR ☐
24 FOUR ☐ 25 NINE ☐ 26 TWENTY THOUSAND ☐
27 THIRTY ☐ 28 THIRTY-NINE ☐ 29 TWENTY-
FOUR ☐ 30 TWO ☐
Your score out of a possible 30:

SUCH COMMON WORDS

1 HONEYMOON ☐ 2 LOVE ☐ 3 CITY ☐ 4 DESERT
☐ 5 WIFE ☐ 6 PARTY ☐ 7 MUSIC ☐ 8 RIVER ☐
9 TRAIN ☐ 10 TOWN ☐ 11 LIFE ☐ 12 LOST ☐
13 COMEDY ☐ 14 HOUSE ☐ 15 FOLLOW ☐
16 MOON ☐ 17 NAKED ☐ 18 ROMANCE ☐
19 GIRL ☐ 20 SONG ☐ 21 AFFAIR ☐ 22 ENEMY ☐
23 GREEN 24 RHYTHM ☐ 25 STAR ☐
Your score out of a possible 25:

FROM THE ORIGINAL STORY

1 GIVE US THIS DAY (US: SALT TO THE DEVIL) ☐
2 ALL ABOUT EVE ☐ 3 STAGECOACH ☐ 4 LADY
FOR A DAY ☐ 5 NIGHT OF THE DEMON (US:
CURSE OF THE DEMON) ☐ 6 FREAKS ☐ 7 SUNSET
BOULEVARD ☐ 8 THE NAKED JUNGLE ☐ 9 THE
MACOMBER AFFAIR ☐ 10 THE FALLEN IDOL ☐
11 IT HAPPENED ONE NIGHT ☐ 12 MR DEEDS
GOES TO TOWN ☐ 13 GUNFIGHT AT THE OK
CORRAL ☐ 14 THE LOST PATROL ☐ 15 TRAP-
EZE ☐ 16 THE PEARL OF DEATH ☐ 17 ISLAND OF

LOST SOULS ☐   18 THE BEAST FROM 20,000 FATHOMS ☐   19 THE THING FROM ANOTHER WORLD ☐   20 SHERLOCK HOLMES FACES DEATH ☐ 21 FOURTEEN HOURS ☐ 22 LOVE FROM A STRANGER ☐

Your score out of a possible 22:

Answer to POSTER 14: 13 WEST STREET ☐

LADDERGRAM 15

ALICIA HUBERMAN is INGRID BERGMAN ☐ in NOTORIOUS ☐
musician LESLIE HOWARD ☐ INTERMEZZO ☐
dowager HELEN HAYES ☐ ANASTASIA ☐
paranoiac ROBERT MONTGOMERY ☐ RAGE IN HEAVEN ☐
adam WARNER BAXTER ☐ ADAM HAD FOUR SONS ☐
neighbour MAY WHITTY ☐ GASLIGHT ☐
oriental ROBERT DONAT ☐ THE INN OF THE SIXTH HAPPINESS ☐
servant FLORA ROBSON ☐ SARATOGA TRUNK ☐
pianist DOOLEY WILSON ☐ CASABLANCA ☐
doctor SPENCER TRACY ☐ DR JEKYLL AND MR HYDE ☐
priest BING CROSBY ☐ THE BELLS OF ST MARY ☐
dentist WALTER MATTHAU ☐ CACTUS FLOWER ☐
businessman CARY GRANT ☐ INDISCREET ☐
mentor YUL BRYNNER ☐ ANASTASIA ☐
Your score out of a possible 28:

COMEBACKS

1 Celia Johnson ☐   2 Pola Negri ☐   3 Janet Gaynor ☐
4 Ethel Barrymore ☐   5 Ed Wynn ☐   6 Alice Faye ☐
7 Constance Bennett ☐   8 Joe E. Brown ☐   9 Ramon Novarro ☐   10 Gloria Swanson ☐   11 Harold Lloyd ☐

12 Henry Fonda ☐ 13 Melvyn Douglas ☐ 14 Anna Sten ☐
15 Elizabeth Bergner ☐ 16 Claudette Colbert ☐ 17 Sylvia
Sidney ☐ 18 Gale Sondergaard ☐ 19 Paul Muni ☐
20 Paulette Goddard ☐ 21 Don Ameche ☐ 22 Myrna
Loy ☐ 23 Jessie Matthews ☐ 24 Al Jolson ☐ 25 Greer
Garson ☐
Your score out of a possible 25:

HEROINES AND HEROES

1 THE RAINS CAME ☐ Myrna Loy ☐ Tyrone Power ☐
2 HOMECOMING ☐ Lana Turner ☐ Clark Gable ☐
3 ALL THIS AND HEAVEN TOO ☐ Bette Davis ☐
Charles Boyer ☐ 4 BRIEF ENCOUNTER ☐ Celia
Johnson ☐ Trevor Howard ☐ 5 DARK VICTORY ☐
Bette Davis ☐ George Brent ☐ 6 THE MAN WHO CAME
TO DINNER ☐ Bette Davis ☐ Richard Travis ☐ 7 THE
LOST WEEKEND ☐ Jane Wyman ☐ Ray Milland ☐
8 MAJOR BARBARA ☐ Wendy Hiller ☐ Rex Harrison ☐
9 THE SHOP AROUND THE CORNER ☐ Margaret
Sullavan ☐ James Stewart ☐ 10 MARTY ☐ Betsy
Blair ☐ Ernest Borgnine ☐ 11 CASABLANCA ☐ Ingrid
Bergman ☐ Humphrey Bogart ☐ 12 ARSENIC AND OLD
LACE ☐ Priscilla Lane ☐ Cary Grant ☐ 13 THE
APARTMENT ☐ Shirley MacLaine ☐ Jack Lemmon ☐
14 THE MIRACLE OF MORGANS CREEK ☐ Betty
Hutton ☐ Eddie Bracken ☐ 15 ON THE WATER-
FRONT ☐ Eva Marie Saint ☐ Marlon Brando ☐ 16 PIC-
NIC ☐ Kim Novak ☐ William Holden ☐ 17 THE QUIET
MAN ☐ Maureen O'Hara ☐ John Wayne ☐ 18 SINGIN'
IN THE RAIN ☐ Debbie Reynolds ☐ Gene Kelly ☐
19 THE MALTESE FALCON ☐ Mary Astor ☐
Humphrey Bogart ☐ 20 TO HAVE AND HAVE NOT ☐
Lauren Bacall ☐ Humphrey Bogart ☐ 21 A STAR IS
BORN ☐ Judy Garland ☐ James Mason ☐ 22 SPELL-
BOUND ☐ Ingrid Bergman ☐ Gregory Peck ☐
23 GUESS WHO'S COMING TO DINNER ☐ Katharine

Houghton ☐ Sidney Poitier ☐ 24 GUYS AND DOLLS ☐
Jean Simmons ☐ Marlon Brando ☐   25 THE GRAD-
UATE ☐ Katharine Ross ☐ Dustin Hoffman ☐ 26 DUEL
IN THE SUN ☐ Jennifer Jones ☐ Gregory Peck ☐
27 DOUBLE INDEMNITY ☐ Barbara Stanwyck ☐
Fred MacMurray ☐   28 CAT PEOPLE ☐ Simone
Simon ☐ Kent Smith ☐   29 BREAKFAST AT TIFF-
ANY'S ☐ Audrey Hepburn ☐ George Peppard ☐ 30 AN
AMERICAN IN PARIS ☐ Leslie Caron ☐ Gene Kelly ☐
Your score out of a possible 90 :

SILENCE PLEASE III

1 Rudolph Valentino ☐ 2 Douglas Fairbanks Jnr ☐ 3 Alan
Crosland ☐ 4 THE COVERED WAGON ☐ 5 NANOOK
OF THE NORTH ☐   6 BLIND HUSBANDS ☐   7 A
CONNECTICUT YANKEE IN KING ARTHUR'S
COURT ☐ 8 PEG O'MY HEART ☐ 9 KRIEMHELD'S
REVENGE ☐   10 THE SORROWS OF SATAN ☐
11 THE MARRIAGE CIRCLE ☐   12 STRIKE ☐
13 Eugenie Besserer ☐ 14 ALOMA OF THE SOUTH
SEAS ☐ 15 Edna Purviance ☐ 16 Adolphe Menjou ☐
17 G. M. 'Broncho Billy' Anderson ☐ 18 NOSFERATU ☐
19 William S. Hart ☐ 20 HEARTS OF THE WORLD ☐
Your score out of a possible 20 :

SWAN SONGS

1 Jean Harlow ☐ 2 Humphrey Bogart ☐ 3 Robert Donat ☐
4 Alan Ladd ☐ 5 Charles Laughton ☐ 6 Buster Keaton ☐
7 John Garfield ☐   8 Carole Lombard ☐   9 Ronald
Colman ☐   10 Gary Cooper ☐   11 John Barrymore ☐
12 Vivien Leigh ☐   13 Lon Chaney ☐   14 Maurice
Chevalier ☐   15 Clifton Webb ☐   16 Spencer Tracy ☐
17 Errol Flynn ☐   18 Edward G. Robinson ☐   19 Claude
Rains ☐ 20 Peter Lorre ☐ 21 Kay Kendall ☐ 22 Sidney

Greenstreet ☐ 23 Montgomery Clift ☐ 24 Paul Douglas ☐
25 Laurence Harvey ☐
Your score out of a possible 25:

BALLETOMANIA

1 THE UNFINISHED DANCE ☐   2 LA MORT DU
CYGNE ☐   3 THE SPECTRE OF THE ROSE ☐
4 Republic ☐   5 Anton Walbrook ☐   6 Monte Carlo ☐
7 KNOCK ON WOOD ☐   8 INVITATION TO THE
DANCE ☐   9 THE MAGIC LAMP ☐   10 THE BAND
WAGON ☐   11 Tamara Toumanova ☐   12 Christopher
Gable ☐
Your score out of a possible 12:

THE SERVANT PROBLEM

1 Gale Sondergaard ☐   2 Judith Anderson ☐   3 Halliwell
Hobbes ☐ 4 Robert Greig ☐ 5 Dirk Bogarde ☐ 6 Seymour
Hicks ☐ 7 Charles Boyer ☐ 8 John Carradine ☐ 9 Boris
Karloff ☐ 10 Richard Haydn ☐ 11 Eric Blore ☐ 12 Willie
Best ☐ 13 Arthur Treacher ☐ 14 Louise Beavers ☐ 15 Stan
Laurel (He really did.) ☐
Your score out of a possible 15:

THE STORYTELLERS

1 Spencer Tracy ☐   2 Michael MacLiammoir ☐   3 Orson
Welles ☐ 4 Orson Welles ☐ 5 Cedric Hardwicke ☐ 6 Orson
Welles ☐   7 Cedric Hardwicke ☐   8 Richard Burton ☐
9 Lionel Barrymore ☐ 10 Victor Jory ☐ 11 Rudy Vallee ☐
12 Walter Pidgeon ☐
Your score out of a possible 12:

CHRISTMAS AT THE MOVIES

1 HOLIDAY INN ☐ 2 BABES IN TOYLAND ☐ 3 Ray
Bolger ☐ 4 Alec Guinness ☐ 5 Reginald Owen ☐ 6 THE

HOLLY AND THE IVY ☐ 7 Humphrey Bogart ☐ Peter Ustinov ☐ Aldo Ray ☐ 8 SCOTT OF THE ANTARC-TIC ☐ 9 BLACK NARCISSUS ☐ 10 CONQUEST OF SPACE ☐ 11 DONOVAN'S REEF ☐ 12 THINGS TO COME ☐ 13 CAMELOT ☐ 14 THE LION IN WINTER ☐ 15 MIRACLE ON 34th STREET ☐
Your score out of a possible 17 :

IT MUST BE LOVE

1 Charles Boyer ☐ Irene Dunne ☐ 2 Ryan O'Neal ☐ Ali MacGraw ☐ 3 Laurence Olivier ☐ Katharine Hepburn ☐ 4 James Cagney ☐ Doris Day ☐ (Cameron Mitchell can be accepted instead of Cagney) 5 Joseph Cotten ☐ Jennifer Jones ☐ 6 Maurice Chevalier ☐ Jeanette MacDonald ☐ 7 Tyrone Power ☐ Loretta Young ☐ 8 Maurice Chevalier ☐ Jeanette MacDonald ☐ 9 William Holden ☐ Jennifer Jones ☐ 10 Glenn Ford ☐ Hope Lange ☐ 11 Don Ameche ☐ Loretta Young ☐ 12 Steve McQueen ☐ Natalie Wood ☐
Your score out of a possible 24 :

Answer to POSTER 15 : JOE MACBETH ☐

ANY COLOUR AS LONG AS IT'S BLACK

1 THE BIRTH OF A NATION ☐ 2 TALES OF MAN-HATTAN ☐ 3 THE EMPEROR JONES ☐ 4 James Baskett ☐ played Uncle Remus ☐ 5 Godfrey Cambridge ☐ 6 His colour was not mentioned ☐ 7 Juano Hernandez ☐ 8 Willie Best ☐ Sleep 'n Eat ☐ 9 UPTIGHT ☐ THE LOST MAN ☐ COOL BREEZE ☐ 10 STORMY WEATHER ☐ 11 William Marshall ☐ 12 Dooley Wilson ☐ 13 Sidney Poitier ☐ Harry Belafonte ☐ Bill Cosby ☐ 14 Hattie McDaniel ☐ 15 Louise Beavers ☐ 16 Cicely Tyson ☐ 17 HALLELUJAH ☐ 18 Paul

Robeson ☐ THE PROUD VALLEY ☐ 19 GET
CHRISTIE LOVE ☐ 20 Stephin Fetchit ☐
Your score out of a possible 27:

MINE, ALL MINE

1 Danny Kaye ☐ 2 Humphrey Bogart ☐ 3 Jack Lemmon ☐
4 John Wayne ☐ 5 Kirk Douglas (it's his mother's name) ☐
6 Raquel Welch and her former husband Patric Curtis ☐
7 Cary Grant ☐ and Stanley Donen 8 Clint Eastwood ☐
10 James Mason (it's his daughter's name) ☐ 11 Frank
Sinatra (spell it backwards) ☐ 12 Alfred Hitchcock ☐
13 Ray Stark ☐ 14 Aaron Rosenberg ☐
Your score out of a possible 14:

REMAKES WITH MUSIC

1 LILIOM ☐ 2 ANNA AND THE KING OF SIAM ☐
3· ACCENT ON YOUTH ☐ 4 TOO MANY HUS-
BANDS ☐ 5 NINOTCHKA ☐ 6 THE SHOP AROUND
THE CORNER ☐ 7 ROOM SERVICE ☐ 8 THE
WOMEN ☐ 9 THE PHILADELPHIA STORY ☐
10 THE MALE ANIMAL ☐ 11 BROTHER RAT ☐
12 BALL OF FIRE ☐
Your score out of a possible 12:

THE CONNECTION

1 Both concerned a search for the truth about a man recently
deceased ☐ 2 Both characters were named Maximilian ☐
3 Both played the obnoxious publicist in different versions of
A STAR IS BORN ☐ 4 O'Herlihy played ROBINSON
CRUSOE, Mantee ROBINSON CRUSOE ON MARS ☐
5 Both included excerpts from silent movies ☐ 6 Both were
based on the old story of the lady who vanished and her
companion who was assured she never existed ☐ 7 Both were
based on novels by Ethel Lina White ☐ 8 R. C. Sheriff

wrote them ☐ James Whale directed them ☐ 9 Both involved Devil's Island ☐ 10 Both involved angels helping people in trouble ☐ 11 James Stewart is the real name of both ☐ 12 Both were photographed by Gregg Toland ☐ 13 The Merry Widow Waltz is central to both ☐ 14 The villain of both films finally falls from a high place ☐ 15 The first scenes of each use subjective camera ☐ 16 Both played Professor Challenger in versions of THE LOST WORLD ☐ 17 A volcanic eruption is the climax of each ☐ 18 The heroine disguises herself as a boy in each case ☐ 19 Both were directed by Julien Duvivier or, if you like, both are composed of episodes ☐ 20 Each plays a villain who commits suicide at the end ☐ 21 The first 3–D film and the first Cinema-Scope film ☐ 22 Both had elevated railway sequences ☐ 23 Both played Oscar Wilde in rival films of 1960 ☐ 24 Both were tentative titles for the film finally released in the US as ARRIVERDERCI BABY and in GB as DROP DEAD DARLING ☐ 25 The first contained a joke about the sledge in the second ☐ 26 Sam Jaffe played an eccentric character part in each ☐ 27 Each involved an airplane crash ☐ 28 Both played Custer ☐ 29 The leading character escapes by air balloon at the end ☐ 30 Both played Bulldog Drummond ☐ 31 Ralph Bellamy is the villain of each ☐ 32 The Devil is a leading figure in each ☐ 33 Both were David O Selznick productions ☐ 34 In both, the title character was never seen ☐ 35 Both had scenes involving a dentist ☐ 36 Both were from novels by Erskine Caldwell ☐ 37 Both concern oversize rabbits ☐ 38 Both take place mainly on a train ☐ 39 Both played the murderer in versions of AND THEN THERE WERE NONE ☐ 40 Both played Micawber in versions of DAVID COPPERFIELD ☐
Your score out of a possible 41 :

PLAY IT AGAIN . . . WITH VARIATIONS

1 SENTIMENTAL JOURNEY ☐   2 THE AWFUL TRUTH ☐ 3 BROADWAY BILL ☐ 4 LADY FOR A

DAY ☐ 5 DARK VICTORY ☐ 6 NOTHING SACRED ☐ 7 FOUR DAUGHTERS ☐ 8 THE MAJOR AND THE MINOR ☐ 9 IT HAPPENED ONE NIGHT ☐ 10 THE FOUR FEATHERS ☐ 11 THE MARRIAGE CIRCLE ☐ 12 THE MILLIONAIRE ☐ 13 LONDON AFTER MIDNIGHT ☐ 14 LIFE BEGINS ☐ 15 IT STARTED WITH EVE ☐ 16 HIGH SIERRA ☐ 17 ROME EXPRESS ☐ 18 MY FAVOUR-ITE WIFE ☐ 19 THE LADY EVE ☐ 20 THE MYSTERY OF THE WAX MUSEUM ☐ 21 THE GHOST BREAKERS ☐ 22 PALEFACE ☐ 23 THIS GUN FOR HIRE ☐ 24 THE INFORMER ☐ 25 THE SEA WOLF ☐ 26 AGAINST ALL FLAGS ☐ 27 RED DUST ☐ 28 AN AMERICAN TRAGEDY ☐ 29 THE CHAMP ☐ 30 TOM DICK AND HARRY ☐ 31 CEIL-ING ZERO ☐ 32 LOVE AFFAIR ☐ 33 EBB TIDE ☐ 34 AH WILDERNESS ☐ 35 THE ASPHALT JUNGLE ☐ 36 THE MALTESE FALCON ☐ 37 SING-APORE ☐ 38 A SLIGHT CASE OF MURDER ☐ 39 DANGEROUS ☐ 40 OUTWARD BOUND ☐
Your score out of a possible 40:

COPYCATS: SECOND DIVISION

1 All played the title characters in films beginning with "I" ☐: I WAS A FUGITIVE FROM A CHAIN GANG ☐ I WAS AN AMERICAN SPY ☐ I WAS A MALE WAR BRIDE ☐ I WAS A COMMUNIST FOR THE FBI ☐ 2 All wrote stories which became Hollywood monster classics ☐: THE INVISIBLE MAN ☐ FRANK-ENSTEIN ☐ DRACULA ☐ DR JEKYLL AND MR HYDE ☐ 3 All played centenarians ☐: THE LOST MOMENT ☐ LITTLE BIG MAN ☐ LOST HORIZON ☐ LOST HORIZON ☐ 4 All appeared together in STAGECOACH ☐ 5 All played Richard III ☐ TOWER OF LONDON 62 ☐ RICHARD III ☐ TOWER OF LONDON 39 ☐ 6 All played leads in films from novels by

Somerset Maugham ☐ CHRISTMAS HOLIDAY ☐ THE MOON AND SIXPENCE ☐ THE RAZOR'S EDGE ☐ OF HUMAN BONDAGE ☐   7 All played Jack the Ripper ☐ A STUDY IN TERROR ☐ THE LODGER ☐ MAN IN THE ATTIC ☐ JACK THE RIPPER ☐   8 All played Nero ☐ THE STORY OF MANKIND ☐ THE SIGN OF THE CROSS ☐ QUO VADIS ☐   9 All played amnesiacs ☐ MISTER BUDDWING ☐ SOMEWHERE IN THE NIGHT ☐ RANDOM HARVEST ☐ MIRAGE ☐   10 All played the lead in CHARLEY'S AUNT ☐ 11 All played Napoleon WATERLOO ☐ WAR AND PEACE or THE YOUNG MR PITT ☐ DESIREE ☐ EAGLE IN A CAGE ☐ 12 All were produced by Howard Hughes ☐ 13 All played opposite Greta Garbo ☐ QUEEN CHRISTINA and several silents ☐ CONQUEST/ MARIE WALEWSKA ☐ NINOTCHKA or TWO-FACED WOMAN ☐ CAMILLE ☐   14 All were played by all-black casts ☐   15 All played D'Artagnan in various versions of THE THREE MUSKETEERS ☐   16 All concerned the Ku Klux Klan ☐ 17 All played dipsomaniacs ☐ SMASH-UP ☐ THE LOST WEEKEND ☐ COME FILL THE CUP ☐ DAYS OF WINE AND ROSES ☐   18 All were made around 1930 in early wide screen systems ☐ 19 All featured Groucho Marx ☐ 20 All played the lead in versions of KISMET ☐ 21 All at various times played The Lone Wolf ☐ 22 All played Lord Nelson ☐ NELSON ☐ LADY HAMILTON ☐ EMMA HAMILTON ☐ A BEQUEST TO THE NATION ☐ 23 Each had two sisters who were also actresses ☐ 24 All played bigamists ☐ THE BIGAMIST ☐ THE REMARKABLE MR PENNY-PACKER ☐ THE CAPTAIN'S PARADISE ☐ THE CONSTANT HUSBAND ☐ 25 All concerned the Foreign Legion ☐ 26 All had climaxes in funfairs ☐ 27 All played Christ ☐ KING OF KINGS 60 ☐ THE GREATEST STORY EVER TOLD ☐ KING OF KINGS 27 ☐ 28 All played Jean Valjean in LES MISERABLES ☐ 29 The hero of each was a multi-murderer ☐   30 Each was remade as a

musical ☐ CAROUSEL ☐ HELLO DOLLY ☐ CABA-RET ☐ THE GIRL MOST LIKELY ☐ 31 All have played Scrooge ☐ 32 All starred Lon Chaney ☐ 33 All went into politics ☐ 34 All had scenes in motels ☐ 35 All were set in San Francisco ☐ 36 All had scenes in sewers ☐ 37 All were uncredited remakes ☐ KISS OF DEATH ☐ THE SEA WOLF ☐ THE LETTER ☐ 38 All were remade from Japanese originals ☐ YOJIMBO ☐ SEVEN SAMURI ☐ RASHOMON ☐ 39 In each case a dual role was involved ☐ 40 All are Laurel and Hardy shorts ☐
Your score out of a possible 103 :

SOME YEARS LATER

1 ON MOONLIGHT BAY ☐ 2 THREE SMART GIRLS GROW UP (THREE SMART GIRLS *is* OK) ☐ 3 ALL QUIET ON THE WESTERN FRONT ☐ 4 CHEAPER BY THE DOZEN ☐ 5 JESSE JAMES ☐ 6 IN THE HEAT OF THE NIGHT ☐ 7 LICENSED TO KILL ☐ 8 DOCTOR NO ☐ 9 A FAMILY AFFAIR (the Hardy family series) ☐ 10 FOUR DAUGHTERS ☐ 11 THE ROBE ☐
Your score out of a possible 11 :

FOR THE VERY FIRST TIME IN THE HISTORY OF THE CINEMA

1 First film in 70mm ☐ 2 First colour feature in 3–D ☐ 3 First British film in colour ☐ 4 First feature in Cinema-Scope ☐ 5 First feature in VistaVision ☐ 6 First film to use the Multiplane camera (which gives depth to cartoons) ☐ 7 First feature in three-colour Technicolor ☐ 8 First Techni-color movie filmed outdoors ☐ 9 First film with talking sequences ☐ 10 First all-talking film ☐ 11 First feature with synchronised sound track ☐ 12 First (and last) film in "Emergo" ☐
Your score out of a possible 12 :

Answer to Poster 16: ONE FOOT IN HELL □

IT ENDED LIKE THIS

1 ACE IN THE HOLE □   2 CASABLANCA □
3 MODERN TIMES □ 4 HARVEY □ 5 ARSENIC AND
OLD LACE □ (He is replying to Cary Grant's assertion
that *he* is the son of a sea cook.)   6 THE THIRD MAN □
7 DUCK SOUP □   8 RANDOM HARVEST □
9 STRANGERS ON A TRAIN □   10 REBECCA □
11 TOP HAT □ 12 THE COUNTRY GIRL □ 13 AND
THEN THERE WERE NONE □ 14 DR NO □ 15 SCAR-
FACE □   16 ALL QUIET ON THE WESTERN
FRONT □   17 ALL THAT MONEY CAN BUY □
18 LOST HORIZON (1937) □   19 HEAVEN CAN
WAIT □ 20 ROOM AT THE TOP □ 21 THE DEVIL
IS A WOMAN (1935) □ 22 THE LADY VANISHES □
23 AFRICAN QUEEN □ 24 THE WOMEN □ 25 THE
BLUE ANGEL □ 26 DEAD OF NIGHT □ 27 ROAD
TO UTOPIA □   28 THE MALTESE FALCON □
29 KIND HEARTS AND CORONETS □   30 THE
WIZARD OF OZ □
Your score out of a possible 30:

LAST LINES

1 LADY IN THE DARK □ Mischa Auer □ 2 HELLZA-
POPPIN □ Elisha Cook Jnr □   3 DESTRY RIDES
AGAIN □ James Stewart □   4 A STAR IS BORN □
Janet Gaynor or Judy Garland □   5 A DAY AT THE
RACES □ Groucho Marx □   6 NORTH BY NORTH-
WEST □ Eva Marie Saint □ Cary Grant □ 7 REBECCA
□ Laurence Olivier □ 8 LITTLE CAESAR □ Edward G.
Robinson □   9 THE GRAPES OF WRATH □ Jane
Darwell □ 10 CASABLANCA □ Humphrey Bogart □
Your score out of a possible 21:

279

LADDERGRAM 16

ALEXANDER HOLLENIUS is CLAUDE RAINS ☐ in
  DECEPTION ☐
young lawyer RICHARD CHAMBERLAIN ☐ TWI-
  LIGHT OF HONOR ☐ (GB: THE CHARGE IS
  MURDER)
Max Corkle JAMES GLEASON ☐ HERE COMES MR
  JORDAN ☐
emperor BRIAN AHERNE ☐ JUAREZ ☐
medical student ROBERT CUMMINGS ☐ KINGS
  ROW ☐
emperor's wife BETTE DAVIS ☐ JUAREZ ☐
singer NELSON EDDY ☐ PHANTOM OF THE
  OPERA ☐
Nazi CONRAD VEIDT ☐ CASABLANCA ☐
werewolf LON CHANEY ☐ THE WOLF MAN ☐
actress MIRIAM HOPKINS ☐ LADY WITH RED
  HAIR ☐
cellist PAUL HENREID ☐ DECEPTION ☐
senator JAMES STEWART ☐ MR SMITH GOES TO
  WASHINGTON ☐
Your score out of a possible 24 :

REAL NAME ROMANCE

1 Jeff Chandler ☐ June Allyson ☐ A STRANGER IN MY
ARMS ☐ 2 Barbara Stanwyck ☐ Kirk Douglas ☐ THE
STRANGE LOVE OF MARTHA IVERS ☐ 3 Marlene
Dietrich ☐ Ray Milland ☐ GOLDEN EARRINGS ☐
4 Ginger Rogers ☐ Cary Grant ☐ ONCE UPON A
HONEYMOON ☐ 5 Cyd Charisse ☐ Fred Astaire ☐
SILK STOCKINGS ☐ 6 Carole Lombard ☐ Jack
Benny ☐ TO BE OR NOT TO BE ☐ 7 Veronica Lake ☐
Fredric March ☐ I MARRIED A WITCH ☐ 8 Susan
Hayward ☐ Rex Harrison ☐ THE HONEY POT ☐
9 Robert Taylor ☐ Jean Harlow ☐ PERSONAL PRO-

PERTY ☐ 10 Joan Crawford ☐ John Garfield ☐ HUMORESQUE ☐ 11 Claire Trevor ☐ John Wayne ☐ STAGECOACH ☐ 12 Jean Arthur ☐ Gary Cooper ☐ MR DEEDS GOES TO TOWN ☐ 13 Jane Wyman ☐ Rock Hudson ☐ MAGNIFICENT OBSESSION ☐ 14 Stewart Granger ☐ Rita Hayworth ☐ SALOME ☐
Your score out of a possible 42:

THE PLOT THICKENS

1 CITIZEN KANE ☐ 2 BLITHE SPIRIT ☐ 3 THE CAT AND THE CANARY ☐ 4 FOREIGN CORRESPONDENT ☐ 5 IT HAPPENED ONE NIGHT ☐ 6 THE LADY VANISHES ☐ 7 KINGS ROW ☐ 8 IT'S A WONDERFUL LIFE ☐ 9 NORTH BY NORTHWEST ☐ 10 THE OLD DARK HOUSE (1932) ☐ 11 NOTHING SACRED ☐ 12 PSYCHO ☐ 13 RANDOM HARVEST ☐ 14 THE MALTESE FALCON ☐ 15 MILDRED PIERCE ☐
Your score out of a possible 15:

TRIPLE TROUBLE II

1 WATERLOO BRIDGE ☐ WATERLOO BRIDGE ☐ GABY ☐ 2 THE DESERT SONG ☐ (all three this title) 3 MADAME X ☐ 4 DADDY LONGLEGS ☐ CURLY TOP ☐ DADDY LONGLEGS ☐ 5 LOVE ☐ ANNA KARENINA ☐ ANNA KARENINA ☐ 6 THE SEA WOLF ☐ BARRICADE ☐ WOLF LARSEN ☐ 7 CLEOPATRA ☐ 8 THE PRISONER OF ZENDA ☐ 9 TO HAVE AND HAVE NOT ☐ THE BREAKING POINT ☐ THE GUN RUNNERS ☐ 10 FOLIES BERGERE ☐ THAT NIGHT IN RIO ☐ ON THE RIVIERA ☐ 11 THE PHANTOM OF THE OPERA ☐ 12 SMILIN' THROUGH ☐ 13 SO BIG ☐ 14 SEVEN KEYS TO BALDPATE ☐ 15

REBECCA OF SUNNYBROOK FARM ☐   16 OF
HUMAN BONDAGE ☐   17 MERTON OF THE
MOVIES ☐ MAKE ME A STAR ☐ MERTON OF THE
MOVIES ☐   18 THE GREAT GATSBY ☐   19 THE
GHOST BREAKER ☐ THE GHOST BREAKERS ☐
SCARED STIFF ☐   20 THE FRONT PAGE ☐ HIS
GIRL FRIDAY ☐ THE FRONT PAGE ☐   21 THE
PHANTOM OF THE OPERA ☐ 22 A CONNECTICUT
YANKEE IN KING ARTHUR'S COURT ☐ 23 BREW-
STER'S MILLIONS ☐ BREWSTER'S MILLIONS ☐
THREE ON A SPREE ☐   24 BACK STREET ☐
25 THE SPOILERS ☐   26 SADIE THOMSON ☐
RAIN ☐ MISS SADIE THOMSON ☐
Your score out of a possible 48:

CLOSING TEST PAPER

1 They were all in 3-D ☐ 2 Mickey Rooney ☐ 3 I CAN
GET IT FOR YOU WHOLESALE ☐ 4 THE THOMAS
CROWN AFFAIR ☐ 5 THE BLACK CAT ☐ 6 DEAD-
LIER THAN THE MALE ☐ 7 SHERLOCK HOLMES
FACES DEATH ☐ 8 NIGHTMARE ☐ 9 THE MILKY
WAY ☐ 10 THEY CALL ME MR TIBBS ☐ 11 Paulette
Goddard ☐   12 Michael Kidd ☐   13 Heydrich ☐
HITLER'S MADMAN ☐ OPERATION DAYBREAK ☐
14 ON THE SPOT ☐ 15 PERSONS IN HIDING ☐
16 PERSONS IN HIDING ☐ UNDERCOVER DOC-
TOR ☐ PAROLE FIXER ☐ QUEEN OF THE MOB ☐
17 Vincent Price ☐ 18 Cedric Hardwicke ☐ 19 Robert
Keith ☐   20 FOUR WIVES ☐ FOUR MOTHERS ☐
21 DAUGHTERS COURAGEOUS ☐ 22 TAILSPIN ☐
23 MAID OF SALEM ☐ Fred MacMurray ☐ Claudette
Colbert ☐ 24 McCABE AND MRS MILLER ☐ 25 Abra-
ham Polonsky ☐ FORCE OF EVIL ☐ John Garfield ☐
26 TUCKER'S PEOPLE ☐ Ira Wolfert ☐ 27 GUILTY
OR INNOCENT: THE SAM SHEPPARD CASE ☐
George Peppard ☐ 28 Ben Gazzara ☐ Anthony Hopkins ☐

29 Jack Hawkins ☐   30 Mia Farrow ☐   31 OUTWARD
BOUND ☐ 32 BETWEEN TWO WORLDS ☐ 33 Sidney
Greenstreet ☐   34 Anne Bancroft ☐   35 Rex Harrison ☐
36 LA BETE HUMAINE ☐   37 Anton Walbrook ☐
38 Max Ophuls ☐ 39 THE BARRETTS OF WIMPOLE
STREET ☐   40 To avoid confusion with the colour re-
make ☐ 41 THE LADY DANCES ☐ 42 Lana Turner ☐
Fernando Lamas ☐ 43 Twentieth Century Fox ☐ 44 PIC-
TURE ☐ Lillian Ross ☐ 45 He played the invisible man,
and became a star on the basis of his voice only ☐ 46 THE
BIRTH OF A NATION ☐ 47 They were Hollywood's most
famous small-part drunks of the thirties ☐   48 Adolf
Hitler ☐   49 Josef Goebbels ☐   50 Henry Wilcoxon ☐
51 The vicar ☐   52 Edmund Gwenn ☐   53 James Dean ☐
54 Anthony Adverse ☐   55 Alan Ladd ☐   56 Groucho
Marx co-authored the first and appeared in the second ☐
57 The vicar ☐ DAVID COPPERFIELD ☐   58 CON-
FLICT ☐   59 Stan Laurel ☐   60 CASABLANCA ☐
Conrad Veidt ☐ Claude Rains ☐   61 THE OLD DARK
HOUSE: she played the centenarian head of the Femm
family, and was credited as John Dudgeon ☐   62 She was
Hollywood's oldest working actress ☐ 63 Estelle Winwood ☐
MURDER BY DEATH ☐   64 Charles Ruggles ☐
65 Lassie ☐ 66 Errol Flynn ☐ 67 They are both pseudo-
nyms of Darryl F. Zanuck ☐ 68 Metro Goldwyn Mayer ☐
69 ESCAPE FROM ZAHRAIN ☐ 70 He was De Mille's
son-in-law ☐   71 THOSE WERE THE DAYS ☐
72 LITTLE MISS MARKER ☐   73 NOW AND FOR-
EVER ☐   74 Henry Hathaway ☐   75 HANGOVER
SQUARE ☐ 76 CHARLEY'S AUNT ☐ Kay Francis ☐
77 I HEARD THE OWL CALL MY NAME ☐
78 Somerset Maugham ☐   79 Paul Gaugin ☐   80 Steve
Geray ☐   81 Doris Dudley ☐   82 MR BELVEDERE
GOES TO COLLEGE ☐ MR BELVEDERE RINGS THE
BELL ☐ 83 CABIN IN THE SKY ☐ 84 SEPTEMBER
AFFAIR; which was made after his death ☐ 85 WHERE'S
CHARLEY ☐ 86 THE SEASHELL AND THE CLERGY-

MAN ☐　87 Reginald Denny ☐　88 Cedric Hardwicke ☐
89 William Dieterle ☐　90 RICH MAN POOR MAN; they
played the leads ☐　91 Francis Lederer ☐　92 THREE
CORNERED MOON ☐　93 THE GRADUATE ☐
94 Claude Rains ☐　95 MOVIN' ON ☐　96 Claude
Akins ☐ Frank Converse ☐ 97 Jules Dassin ☐ 98 Graham
Moffatt ☐ Moore Marriott ☐　99 Arthur Askey ☐
100 Rouben Mamoulian ☐　101 Michael Winner ☐
102 a. MACMILLAN AND WIFE ☐ b. COLUMBO ☐
c. FARADAY AND COMPANY ☐ d. McCOY ☐
e. McCLOUD ☐ f. BANACEK ☐　103 OPERATION
PETTICOAT ☐　104 I WAS A MALE WAR BRIDE ☐
105 THE PAJAMA GAME ☐　106 John Raitt ☐
107 PEYTON PLACE ☐ 108 KINGS ROW ☐ 109 THE
KREMLIN LETTER ☐　110 Bela Lugosi ☐　111 ONCE
UPON A TIME ☐　112 Ted Donaldson ☐　113 Loretta
Young ☐　114 Robert Williams ☐　115 Franklin Schaff-
ner ☐ 116 MADAME SATAN ☐ 117 TALES OF MAN-
HATTAN ☐ 118 FLESH AND FANTASY ☐ 119 Julien
Duvivier ☐　120 THE PAJAMA GAME ☐　121 Ian
Fleming ☐　122 Dennis Hoey ☐　123 THE PEARL OF
DEATH ☐　124 George Zucco ☐　125 Henry Daniell ☐
126 Edward Van Sloan ☐　127 Dwight Frye ☐　128
FREAKS ☐ 129 Virginia Weidler ☐ 130 Robert Donat ☐
131 Robert Morley ☐　132 Spencer Tracy ☐　133 Marcel
Carne ☐　134 Cinematography ☐　135 Musical scoring ☐
136 Anton Karas ☐　137 THE GHOST STORY ☐
138 SCARED STIFF ☐ 139 Boris Karloff: he could not be
released from his stage contract ☐　140 BICYCLE
THIEVES ☐　141 THE MAN WHO TALKED TOO
MUCH ☐ ILLEGAL ☐　142 Joseph Schildkraut ☐
143 Innokenti Smoktunovsky ☐　144 GO INTO YOUR
DANCE ☐ Ruby Keeler ☐ 145 Rex Beach ☐ 146 Anne
Baxter ☐　147 I CLAUDIUS ☐　148 The Falcon ☐
149 Mel Blanc ☐　150 Night clubs ☐　151 Claudette
Colbert ☐ 152 Asses' milk ☐ 153 Alan Young ☐ 154 Leo
Genn ☐　155 Whither goest thou? ☐　156 Danger ☐

157 Ruth Etting ☐   158 LOVE ME OR LEAVE ME ☐
159 Eight million ☐   160 Michael Powell ☐ and Emeric
Pressburger ☐; they wrote, produced and directed their
films ☐ 161 Madeleine Smith ☐ Ann Todd ☐ 162 Phyllis
Calvert ☐ Stewart Granger ☐   163 THE THING FROM
ANOTHER WORLD ☐   164 Dorothy Comingore ☐
165 Paul Stewart ☐ 166 Xanadu ☐ 167 Colonel Haki ☐
168 Patsy Ruth Miller ☐ 169 Maureen O'Hara ☐ 170 Gina
Lollobrigida ☐   171 Billie Burke ☐   172 The God in
ZARDOZ was named after the wiZARD of OZ ☐   173 A
RAGE TO LIVE ☐   174 THE FOUR FEATHERS ☐
175 A. E. W. Mason ☐   176 Russell Simpson ☐
177 Twentieth Century Fox ☐   178 SON OF KONG ☐
179 Sidney Greenstreet ☐ 180 Peter Lorre ☐ 181 PRINCE
VALIANT ☐   182 Elissa Landi ☐   183 William Friese-
Greene ☐   184 Laurence Olivier ☐   185 A New York cop,
original hero of the exploits portrayed in THE FRENCH
CONNECTION ☐ 186 A famous Hollywood art director ☐
187 A Hollywood dress designer ☐   188 They have both
played DILLINGER in films of that name ☐   189 Walter
Lang ☐   190 John Farrow ☐   191 PRIDE AND PRE-
JUDICE ☐   192 They were all Mack Sennett Bathing
Beauties ☐ 193 Eleanor Powell ☐ 194 THE GREAT MAN
VOTES ☐   195 Carol Reed ☐   196 Edna May Oliver ☐
197 Lon Chaney Jnr ☐   198 Glenn Strange ☐   199 John
Carradine ☐   200 Jessie Ralph ☐   201 Herbert Mundin ☐
202 Jessie Ralph ☐ 203 Marie Dressler ☐ 204 Wheeler and
Woolsey ☐   205 May Robson ☐   206 It was written as a
Perry Mason adventure by Erle Stanley Gardner ☐
207 GREED ☐   208 Jean Hersholt ☐ Gibson Gowland ☐
209 HAPPY BIRTHDAY WANDA JUNE ☐   210 Rita
Hayworth ☐   211 San Francisco ☐   212 THE AFRICAN
QUEEN ☐   213 MY FAVOURITE BLONDE ☐
214 SULLIVAN'S TRAVELS ☐   215 Erik Rhodes ☐
THE GAY DIVORCE ☐   216 LOST HORIZON ☐
217 THE MIRACLE OF MORGAN'S CREEK ☐
218 Charlton Heston ☐   219 Miles Mander ☐   220 Rene

Clair ☐ 221 Zoltan Korda ☐ 222 Roland Young ☐ 223 Donald Ogden Stewart ☐ 224 They have all played the lead in CHARLEY'S AUNT or variations of it ☐ 225 GRAND HOTEL ☐ 226 HOLLYWOOD PARTY ☐ 227 GRAND HOTEL ☐ Greta Garbo ☐ 228 CHARADE ☐ 229 THE IRON CURTAIN ☐ 230 Vittorio de Sica ☐ 231 James Finlayson ☐ 232 Edgar Kennedy ☐ 233 Charles Hall ☐ 234 Jean Hersholt ☐ 235 Josef Von Sternberg ☐ 236 Rosalind Russell ☐ Douglas Fairbanks Jnr ☐ Maureen O'Sullivan ☐ 237 The role in FOLIES BERGERE which was rewritten for THAT NIGHT IN RIO and ON THE RIVIERA ☐ 238 Rex Ingram ☐ 239 Richard Basehart ☐ 240 THE GARDEN OF ALLAH ☐ 241 Mr Magoo in FUDDY DUDDY BUDDY ☐ 242 FOREIGN CORRES-PONDENT ☐ 243 William Demarest ☐ 244 Fay Holden ☐ 245 Lionel Barrymore ☐ 246 Jill Haworth ☐ 247 Walter Huston ☐ 248 Victor McLaglen ☐ Edmund Lowe ☐ 249 Noel Coward ☐ 250 Pat O'Brien ☐ 251 Three ☐ 252 Virginia Bruce ☐ Joan Fontaine ☐ Susannah York ☐ 253 They were all members of the original OUR GANG ☐ 254 Ann Rutherford ☐ 255 Warner's great art director of the thirties ☐ 256 Michael Sarrazin ☐ 257 GUNSMOKE: he was James Arness ☐ 258 Dan Dailey ☐ 259 Helen Hayes ☐ Mildred Natwick ☐ 260 Paulette Goddard ☐ 261 Lewis Stone ☐ 262 Ramon Novarro ☐ Douglas Fairbanks Jnr ☐ James Mason ☐ 263 DUCK SOUP ☐ 264 THE BANK DICK ☐ 265 No: he was not in THE BIG STORE ☐ 266 CHEYENNE AUTUMN ☐ 267 LOVE ME TO-NIGHT ☐ 268 Fred Zinnemann ☐ 269 The Crazy Gang ☐ 270 ☐☐ Any two of OK FOR SOUND, ALF'S BUTTON AFLOAT, GASBAGS, THE FROZEN LIMITS, LIFE IS A CIRCUS 271 Kenneth More ☐ REACH FOR THE SKY ☐ 272 THE LOST WORLD ☐ 273 She played their landlady ☐ 274 Joe E. Brown ☐ 275 Leon Errol ☐ MEXICAN SPITFIRE ☐ 276 Olive Oyl ☐ 277 William Castle ☐ 278 THE BEST YEARS OF

OUR LIVES ☐   279 Turhan Bey ☐   280 Paramount's famous art director of the thirties ☐

Your score out of a possible 328 :

PICTURE QUIZ

1 Toto ☐ THE HARVEY GIRLS ☐ He's Ray Bolger ☐ Frank Morgan ☐ His brother, Ralph Morgan ☐ THE NIGHT THEY RAIDED MINSKY'S ☐ Tin Man Jack Haley ☐ His son married Judy Garland's daughter Liza ☐ L. Frank Baum ☐   2 THE GHOST OF FRANKEN-STEIN ☐ Lon Chaney Jnr ☐ Evelyn Ankers ☐ Cedric Hardwicke ☐ Bela Lugosi ☐ Ygor ☐ 3 Ernest Borgnine ☐ Bette Davis ☐ BUNNY O'HARE ☐ THE CATERED AFFAIR ☐   4 CHARLEY'S AUNT ☐ Brandon Thomas ☐ Arthur Askey ☐ Charlie Ruggles ☐ Jack Benny ☐ Ray Bolger ☐ Felix Aylmer ☐ MR EMMAN-UEL ☐ 5 Tony Curtis ☐ SOME LIKE IT HOT ☐ Joe E. Brown ☐ "Nobody's perfect" ☐ Marilyn Monroe ☐ 6 James Mason ☐ Barbara Mullen ☐ Margaret Lock-wood ☐ A PLACE OF ONE'S OWN ☐ Osbert Sitwell ☐ 7 Roland Young ☐ THE MAN WHO COULD WORK MIRACLES ☐ AND THEN THERE WERE NONE ☐ Uriah Heep ☐ Ralph Richardson ☐ HOME AT SEVEN (US: MURDER ON MONDAY) ☐ 8 Juano Hernandez ☐ Paul Newman ☐ Richard Beymer ☐ HEMINGWAY'S ADVENTURES OF A YOUNG MAN ☐ INTRUDER IN THE DUST ☐ Elizabeth Patterson ☐ Claude Jarman Jnr ☐ THE SILVER CHALICE ☐ WEST SIDE STORY ☐ 9 Tony Randall ☐ SEVEN FACES OF DR LAO ☐ 10 Rock Hudson ☐ SECONDS ☐ John Franken-heimer ☐ John Hamilton ☐ PRETTY MAIDS ALL IN A ROW ☐ 11 Patrick McGoohan ☐ DR SYN ALIAS THE SCARECROW ☐ Walt Disney ☐ George Arliss ☐ Peter Cushing ☐ DR SYN ☐ CAPTAIN CLEGG or NIGHT CREATURES ☐ Russell Thorndike ☐ 12 J. Carrol Naish ☐

HOUSE OF FRANKENSTEIN ☐ 13 Who said Karloff? It's Glenn Strange ☐ GUNSMOKE ☐ 14 Jack Gifford ☐ Michael Hordern ☐ Zevo Mostel ☐ Phil Silvers ☐ A FUNNY THING HAPPENED ON THE WAY TO THE FORUM ☐ Richard Lester ☐ 15 Dick Van Dyke ☐ Billy Bright ☐ THE COMIC ☐ 16 Red Buttons ☐ Peter Lorre ☐ Barbara Eden ☐ Cedric Hardwicke ☐ Fabian ☐ Richard Haydn ☐ FIVE WEEKS IN A BALLOON ☐ Irwin Allen ☐ Jules Verne ☐ 17 Joan Crawford ☐ Rossano Brazzi ☐ THE STORY OF ESTHER COSTELLO ☐ THE GOLDEN VIRGIN ☐ Heather Sears ☐ 18 Adam West ☐ Burt Ward ☐ Burgess Meredith ☐ the Penguin ☐ Cesar Romero ☐ the Joker ☐ Frank Gorshin ☐ the Riddler ☐ Lee Meriwether ☐ the Catwoman ☐ 19 The Jones Family ☐ Kenneth Lake ☐ Jed Prouty ☐ Spring Byington ☐ Florence Roberts ☐ 20 Rondo Hatton ☐ The Creeper ☐ 21 E. E. Clive ☐ Edward Brophy ☐ Edward Arnold ☐ Edward Arnold ☐ THE LAST HURRAH ☐ DIAMOND JIM ☐ LILLIAN RUSSELL ☐ REMEMBER LAST NIGHT? ☐

Your score out of a possible 119 :

YOUR GRAND TOTAL :